Two Shall Be One

C. M. WARD

TWO SHALL BE ONE

C. M. Ward

Copyright © 1986 by
C. M. Ward

Printed in the United States of America
ISBN: 0-88368-184-6

Editorial assistance by Valeria Cindric.

DEDICATION

This book is dedicated to my wife Dorothy, who, through years of demanding assignments and hours of duty, has managed to keep our marriage fresh and romantic. She is living proof that it can be done—and enjoyed while doing it.

Dorothy is a domestic artist. Her touch can turn any house into a palace; her cooking makes any meal a gourmet's delight. Her choice of clothing and accessories have always made me proud to have my wife by my side.

During our sixty years of married life, I have had many opportunities to practice what I preach. And Dorothy has been an excellent coach! If I do not graduate from the school of marriage *summa cum laude*, it will not be her fault.

Dorothy means "gift from God." As my loving companion and enthusiastic supporter, my wife has certainly lived up to her name. She is my special gift from God.

If this book blesses you, please thank her!

CONTENTS

FOREWORD

by Jim Bakker

The battle for the family has begun. Today, the enemy's batallions have united in strength to launch an all-out attack on our most sacred and precious institution—marriage.

Dr. Ward's TWO SHALL BE ONE is a much-needed survival and success manual for those who are married and those contemplating marriage.

Within these pages, Dr. Ward has combined his invaluable insight with sound biblical truth gained through his lifelong study of Scripture. His profundity and humor combine to make TWO SHALL BE ONE delightful, enlightening, and life-changing.

For years, I listened to the *Revivaltime* voice of C. M. and have since invited him to speak on countless occasions at Heritage, USA. He is a godly man, a loyal friend, a wise adviser, and, most significantly, a man who has faithfully applied the principles of God's Word to his own marriage and family. I have long waited for his wisdom on the subject to be recorded in a book.

Here are the "how to's" and the "what not to do's" of love and marriage—practical suggestions, personal experiences, and possible pitfalls. In his treasure of truths, Dr. Ward reveals the success formula for a godly marriage and a happy home.

At last, a practical book for husbands and wives from one of America's best-loved preachers. Here are the secrets that *will* work in your marriage.

Jim Bakker
President, PTL Television Network

18.   And the Lord God said, It is not good that the man should be alone; I will make him an help meet for him. . . .

21.   And the Lord God caused a deep sleep to fall upon Adam, and he slept: and he took one of his ribs, and closed up the flesh instead thereof;

22.   And the rib, which the Lord God had taken from man, made he a woman, and brought her unto the man.

23.   And Adam said, This is now bone of my bones, and flesh of my flesh: she shall be called Woman, because she was taken out of Man.

24.   Therefore shall a man leave his father and his mother, and shall cleave unto his wife: and they shall be one flesh.

1
IT TAKES TWO

"I do." No two words have had more impact on individual lives, and society as a whole, than these. You may have repeated them at the altar yourself, or if not, you probably will someday.

My wife Dorothy and I said "I do" to one another on Christmas Day, 1929, a few weeks after the stock crash. Beginning a marriage during our nation's worst financial and economic crisis was quite a challenge for two young people. I had just completed Bible college, and we had been asked to pastor in a northern Canadian community where there was not a single convert. We had no money and no source to turn to except God.

Our first convert was a young man who, thankfully, had a job. I led him to Christ, and Dorothy convinced him to become our boarder. We managed to live on the five dollars a week he paid us. Later, our situation improved when a farmer and his family were saved. That meant we had milk, cream, butter, eggs, and occasionally a chicken to eat!

Such circumstances sound more like grounds for divorce than the foundation for a successful marriage. But adversity often lays the groundwork for a strong and lasting relationship—especially when you are determined to work at building a life together. Although those first few years of our marriage were tough, Dorothy and I dug in and never looked back.

I have always liked what Satchel Page, the famous baseball pitcher, called a cardinal rule of life, "Never look back, something may be gaining on you." That's good advice for any relationship.

There are times, however, when looking back has its advantages. Let's take a glance back through history and see if we can shed some light on this complicated subject of marriage.

What Is Marriage?

Anthropologists define marriage as "a relation of one or more men to one or more women that is recognized by custom or law and involves certain rights and duties." This general definition makes room for many different interpretations—from polygamy in the Old Testament to celibate marriages among priests and nuns during the middle ages.

In times past, getting two people married involved intricate social customs. Some cultures enlisted the aid of a matchmaker to find a partner for their marriageable son or daughter. Remember the musical "Fiddler On The Roof"? Even today in many eastern cultures, families arrange the details of a marriage without consulting the young man and woman involved.

No wonder elopement became popular. This practice originated in Europe when a woman's father promised her to a man she didn't like. To avoid the arranged marriage, the engaged woman ran away with her true lover.

Marriage-by-capture was a more forceful way of making sure your son married the right girl. After the bride was abducted, she and the groom remained in hiding until the girl's parents gave up the search. Thus the inception of what is today called the honeymoon.

The fact that today's parents are expected to foot the bill for the wedding goes back to the days of payment. What strange practices this arrangement of marriage has encountered—barter, dowry, purchase!

In our modern, sophisticated society, marriage is not a cultural or a family decision. You are not drafted into marriage—it is a choice you make of your own free will. No law, divine or civil, says you *have* to get married. Entering into marriage is a voluntary, individual act.

Maybe we need to take a second look at what the marriage ceremony really means. Is it just the public acknowledgement of a man and woman's decision to live together? Do we go through the motions just to satisfy the legal requirements and fulfill our social obligations?

While the marriage ceremony is usually performed before relatives and friends, getting married is a very personal experience. "I . . . take thee . . . to be my lawfully, wedded wife." Marriage takes a life—"I take thee." Nothing is more serious than that. It is the most important temporal commitment anyone will ever make.

The Marriage Contract

When two people repeat their vows at the altar, they make many promises to one another. A promise is an extension of credit—an "I.O.U." The church and state are actually extending credit for a couple to strengthen society under specific guidelines. If either party ignores or abuses such credit, he or she is guilty of fraud.

Because the marriage contract is one of the most binding agreements ever sanctioned by society, it cannot be entered into lightly or abridged impulsively. The moment the agreeing parties attach their signatures to a license, the marriage contract is in force. Waiting until the act of physical intercourse occurs is not necessary. This contract immediately becomes as legally binding as any mortgage or loan agreement, and the responsibility for payment begins at once!

"Until death us do part" is the only statute of limitations read during the wedding ceremony. To voluntarily enter a marriage contract and not plan on keeping your end of the bargain is illegal and immoral. Couples who want marriage on a short-term basis should "pledge their troth" (take an oath) to fulfill their vows for the designated length of time. The Bible explicitly says it is better not to vow a vow than to vow a vow and not keep it. (See Ecclesiastes 5:5.)

To renege means "to go back on a promise or commitment, to revoke" (Webster). God says, "If any man draws back, my soul shall have no pleasure in him" (Hebrews 10:38). Jesus said, "No man, having put his hand to the plough, and looking back, is fit for the kingdom of God" (Luke 9:62).

Full Partners

Sometimes, my wife Dorothy teasingly says, "Remember, you were not the only pebble on the beach!"

To that I reply, "You are right, but I was the only one who signed the contract!"

Marriage is designed to be a long and unfolding agreement between two partners. It is a contract of *partnership,* not a contract of *ownership*—neither party owns the other.

This partnership is an agreement to pursue common goals. Establishing a home, building a relationship, and producing a family take first priority. Later, the partnership enjoys the fruit of labor, pursues mutually oriented activities, and strengthens the community.

In order for this relationship to grow and deepen, mutual trust is absolutely necessary. Without the security of long-range commitment, a couple may speak of their living arrangement or social adjustment but not of their marriage.

We need trust and support from our partners if we are going to have the strength to deal with our own limitations and fears. "Two are better than one; because they have a good reward for their labour. For if they fall, the one will lift up his fellow: but woe to him that is alone when he falleth; for he hath not another to help him up" (Ecclesiastes 4:9-10).

One husband plus one wife may legally constitute a marriage, but that doesn't necessarily make two people one flesh. God said: "A man . . .

shall cleave unto his wife: and they *shall be* one flesh" (Genesis 2:24, italics mine). Becoming one doesn't happen automatically. Instead, it takes years of effort and the determination to stick together.

The adhesive in marriage is *commitment*—"with all my heart." Commitment takes more than a simple "I do"—it requires faith and two people willing to make it work no matter what the cost.

If you have that kind of stick-to-itiveness, then let me share with you some practical ways *two* people can become *one*—with God's help.

22. Wives, submit yourselves unto your own husbands, as unto the Lord.

23. For the husband is the head of the wife, even as Christ is the head of the church: and he is the saviour of the body.

24. Therefore as the church is subject unto Christ, so let the wives be to their own husbands in everything. . . .

33. Nevertheless let every one of you in particular so love his wife even as himself; and the wife see that she reverence her husband.

2

ONE PLUS ONE

Every marriage involves *two* personalities—his and hers. The miracle of marriage happens when these two distinct personalities are sublimated to work together in a harmonious relationship.

The first week after we were married, I said to my young wife, "Dorothy, you don't cook like my mother cooks."

Her reply set the tone for our relationship, "And you don't dress me like my father dressed me!"

This element of healthy competition between Dorothy and I has added fun and sizzle to our marriage. There is only one problem—she wins any game we play, from Rook to Scrabble!

Early in our married life we learned to complement each other instead of fighting the differences. The matter of finances is a good example. I have always been the money-maker, and Dorothy has been the money-manager. We each use our God-given talents and abilities for the benefit of our partnership.

In any marriage, the first step to compatability is recognizing the differences between partners. The simple fact that men are men and women are women automatically brings two unique personality types to the relationship.

Men are duty bound and work oriented. From childhood, they have been taught the obligation of "doing the chores"—carrying out the garbage, washing the car, mowing the lawn, etc.

To a woman, the sheer pleasure of spending time together often comes before keeping a schedule or performing a task. Wives want the same lingering, listening, and looking into one another's eyes that went on during courtship.

Intimacy means one thing to a woman and something quite different to a man. The only closeness a husband may need is having his wife work next to him in the garden. Intimacy to a wife, however, means being alone together in a romantic setting where everyday cares are forgotten.

Women enjoy conversation while men are inclined to be silent partners. Sharing experiences and making small talk are important to a woman. I know men who avoid any kind of conversation with their wives because they feel intimidated or foolish about discussing simple, everyday matters.

Men have a tendency to draw apart and isolate themselves. Some husbands would rather spend all day Saturday alone in a fishing boat than at home with their wife. By contrast, women seldom do things by themselves. If her husband won't go shopping with her, a wife will call a girlfriend to go along. Husbands need to remember that at the slightest lack of attention, some women can quickly feel neglected and abandoned.

Marriage inclines a woman toward her parents, but the opposite is generally true for a man. A husband may feel cheated by the closeness his wife shares with her family, but he must understand that she needs her parents' approval. A woman is proud to carry her "report card" home and show them how well she is doing. Husbands, on the other hand, like to appear independent of their parents. For this reason, men often avoid a close relationship with them once they are married.

Male and female temperaments are also very different. In most cases, the husband is inclined to be optimistic while the wife tends to be the worrier. "How are we going to pay the bills? The children are ready to go to college. What would happen if you died?" Most of the time, husbands must buoy their wives and assure them that everything will be all right.

The unique personalities of a husband and wife should contribute to a successful marriage—not destroy it. Don't try to make each other over. Clones are not exciting. Attempting to run your mate through the same mold you were cut from will result in a boring, drab relationship.

Matched And Mismatched

Different combinations of personality types make numerous marital arrangements possible. During my years of pastoring and counseling, I have noticed these nine possible husband-wife categories. You may find your marriage in one of them, or yours may be a combination of two or more arrangements.

1. *The husband is the leader—but detached.*

In this type of marriage, the wife is frustrated and helpless. Instead of confronting difficult situations, the husband withdraws and refuses to take any initiative in family affairs. The wife has learned to hold *in* and hold *back,* accepting security without pleasure and making a personal sacrifice for the welfare of the children.

This type of husband-wife arrangement is reflected in the Jacob-Leah marriage. (See Genesis 29.)

2. *The husband is the leader—but aggressive and combative.*

A marriage of this kind leaves little room for effective communication. The loud, abusive bully of a husband boasts that he "wears the pants" in the family. His wife, on the other hand, sandpapers this macho image by nagging. She has learned to sidestep his authority and knows that he is not as sure of himself as he pretends to be.

The Nabal-Abigail contract is a good study in this kind of marital arrangement. (See 1 Samuel 25.)

3. *The husband is the leader—with a negative attitude.*

This kind of man approaches every situation on the defensive. His lack of self-esteem forces him to use put-downs and derogatory remarks in order to maintain his position of authority in the home. As the recipient of her husband's abuse, the wife is critical of his decisions and seldom supports him. Whenever they are in public, she uses every opportunity to humiliate her husband before others.

David and his first wife, Michal, are an example of how this type of negativism can destroy a marriage. (See 2 Samuel 6:12-23.)

4. *The husband is the leader—with a charming personality.*

This guy is a good *family man* who always tries to make the home a fun place. He believes laughter is the cure for most wrinkles in marriage. His wife thinks he is wonderful and has built her entire life around him. Unfortunately, because she never fully develops her own personality or potential, she may come to resent her husband as they grow older.

Many of these elements are seen in the relationship between Isaac and Rebekah. (See Genesis chapters 24-27.)

5. *The husband is the leader—with a super-submissive wife.*

The husband is obviously in control, and he seldom consults his wife on important matters. She has been taught the way a wife *should* behave and accepts her husband's decisions without question. This kind of super-submissive wife, however, tends to have a low self-image and a self-righteous attitude.

The tie between Abraham and Sarah reflects a marital arrangement involving these two personality types. (See Genesis 12.)

6. *The wife is the leader—with a take-charge attitude.*

The hen-pecked husband in this kind of

marriage is always the minor influence in the home. His wife rules the roost in a shrill, demanding, and resourceful manner. To get her way she uses the "cold shoulder" and the "hot tongue." Because he has been conditioned to avoid conflict, the husband forfeits his leadership role and takes the path of least resistance.

Examine the Ahab-Jezebel coupling to see how this arrangement works. (See 1 Kings 21.)

7. *The wife is the leader—by default.*

In this marriage, both partners are insecure. The husband, a sort of namby-pamby mamma's boy who never quite reached manhood, goes his own way with as little fuss as possible. His lack of ambition to get ahead causes his wife to fear for the financial stability of the home. To motivate him to be a man, she uses a pushy and intrusive manner—but with little success.

This may have been the case in the marriage of Ananias and Sapphira. (See Acts 5.)

8. *The wife is the leader—in a congenial situation.*

This couple maintains a low-key relationship by not making excessive demands on each other. Because the husband is successful and secure, he is not competitive and takes pride in his wife's accomplishments. She has a take-charge attitude combined with a deep sense of respect for her husband and his position.

This arrangement is seen in the home of Elizabeth and Zacharias. (See Luke chapter 1.)

9. *Husband is the leader—in a sharing relationship.*

In the ideal marriage, the husband's loving leadership is supported by a wife who respects his position as head of the home. Within their respective roles, husband and wife share family responsibilities. He takes pride in his work and is a good provider. As manager of the household, the wife uses her talents to meet the needs of the family. Husband and wife exchange views and respect each other's opinions. At the heart of this sharing relationship is a deep spiritual oneness that brings stability and unity to their home and marriage.

Aquila and Priscilla had this kind of give-and-take marriage. (See Acts 18:1-3,26; Romans 16:3-5.) Let's take a closer look at this last couple and see why their marriage was such a success.

The Ideal Couple

As we look into this famous couple's past, we find that their backgrounds were quite different. Aquila was a Jewish believer from Pontus—a remote land on the shore of the Black Sea at the perimeter of civilization. Priscilla, a name that indicates aristocracy, was probably a Roman woman of high social standing. The bonds of Christ, however, were sufficient to bring together these extremes in culture and social status.

Aquila was a hardworking missionary whose name means the *eagle*. Like most missionaries, he led a wandering life moving from one city to another. We read of him first at Pontus, then at Rome, later at Corinth and Ephesus, then back to Rome and at Ephesus again.

In spite of their gypsy-like lifestyle, Priscilla always followed her husband. My wife Dorothy has this same kind of flexible nature. On our many evangelistic and mission tours, we have had accomodations that were far below our normal standards of convenience and cleanliness. But Dorothy always adjusted to any situation like a trooper. Priscilla, too, must have faced many difficult situations with a stiff upper lip.

During one of the first Jewish persecutions, Aquila was expelled from Rome. At that point, Priscilla's loyalty to her husband may have been tested, but she was determined to follow him, if need be, to the ends of the earth.

When this devoted couple came to Corinth, they started a tentmaking business. The apostle

Paul had also come to this sinful, pagan city, and he needed a job. It was probably at a fellowship meeting of the local believers that Paul met Aquila and Priscilla. He joined them in their tentmaking business and soon a strong, committed friendship developed. It wasn't long before Paul viewed this couple as "my helpers in Christ Jesus" (Romans 16:3).

When Paul decided to go to Ephesus, Aquila and Priscilla liquidated their prosperous business and accompanied him. With their assets, they invested in a spacious home and began a "church . . . in their house" (Romans 16:5). They unselfishly opened their home to neighbors and started having services. Think of the sacrifice involved as Priscilla put the cause of Jesus Christ ahead of her furniture, her privacy, and her security. She wanted her home to be used for the work of the gospel.

Paul pays high tribute to Aquila and Priscilla, saying that they were willing to "lay down their . . . necks" to save his life (Romans 16:4). Ten years later, some of Paul's fellow-workers had fallen away, but not these two. In his final letter, the apostle bids farewell to his friends, "Salute Prisca and Aquila" (2 Timothy 4:19).

Their witness for Jesus remained firm, and their marriage testified to the strong bond of love and unity between them. Whenever they are mentioned in the New Testament, their names are always found together: "Aquila and Priscilla," or "Priscilla and Aquila."

God's Ideal For Marriage

Why is it that some couples have successful marriages while others are obvious failures? Are there certain principles that guarantee a happy and successful marital relationship?

To discover God's ideal for marriage we must look back to Eden. The garden marriage involved two people who were sinless and innocent in their love and enjoyment of each other. Adam and Eve had the makings for a perfect marriage—no outside pressures, no meddling in-laws, no financial worries, not even a diaper to change.

It was the ideal situation. As long as Adam and Eve adhered to God's plan, neither experienced a tired wrinkle or a frown on their flawless, innocent faces. But the sweet-talking serpent crept into this tranquil setting and tempted Eve to sin.

Suddenly everything changed, and Adam and Eve found themselves hiding from God. Worry and anxiety entered their lives and permeated their blissful existence. For the first time, Adam spoke to his wife in anger, and Eve coldly rebuffed her husband's caresses. They both experienced a touch of hell.

Adam blamed Eve for his transgression—"The woman . . . she gave me of the tree." Although Scripture states that Eve was deceived, it's clear that Adam knew exactly what he was doing. (See 1 Timothy 2:14.) He made a calculated decision and voluntarily joined in his wife's sin.

Adam, knowing that the consequence was death, chose to risk alienation from God rather than separation from Eve. That may sound chivalrous on Adam's part, but his motives were probably more selfish than noble.

On that day, Adam and Eve did not immediately die. Something far worse happened: they "began to die." Their beautiful marital relationship—the best this planet has even seen—began to fall apart.

When Adam and Eve stumbled out of Eden, the only institution they brought with them was marriage. But how can marriage survive in a fallen world when living in paradise didn't guarantee success?

Two verses give us a glimpse into God's ideal for the marriage relationship. Although Eve was deceived, the Lord did not excuse her sin. "And the Lord God said unto the woman, What is this that thou hast done?" (Genesis 3:13). Her husband was also rebuked by the Lord, but for a different reason. Adam had hearkened "unto the voice" of his wife (verse 17).

God had expected Adam to exercise leadership in the marriage relationship, and Eve was supposed to support her husband in that role. When things got turned around, the result was chaos, confusion, and disaster.

In order for marriage to work, *leadership must be exercised by the male.* This is not to imply that man does not benefit from the counsel and talent of his "help meet." A husband needs help—all the help he can get. But there can be only *one* leader in a marriage, and God's Word makes it very clear which partner that is to be.

"But I would have you know, that the head of every man is Christ; and the head of the woman is the man. . . . For the man is not of the woman; but the woman of the man. Neither was the man created for the woman; but the woman for the man" (1 Corinthians 11:3,8-9).

Man needs a woman. Without a woman, a man could never be in love. Without a wife, he could never be a husband or a father. "Nevertheless neither is the man without the woman, neither the woman without the man, in the Lord. For as the woman is of the man, even so is the man also by the woman; but all things of God" (verses 11-12).

Because the husband is held responsible by God, he must place his commitment to God above the marriage relationship. Neither love, family, nor fidelity provide an excuse for man's spiritual rebellion. The most difficult choice a husband has to make is to put God absolutely first, regardless of the consequences.

We could all be living in paradise if Adam had insisted upon submission and repentance instead of abjectly surrendering to his wife's deceit and rebellion. No marriage or home can survive with disobedience as its foundation.

The husband must maintain the spiritual authority in the home or lose his God-given position. "As for me and my house, we will serve the Lord" (Joshua 24:15) should be the motto of every Christian husband and father.

Unequally Yoked

One of the most significant criteria for a happy marriage can be determined even before you make the choice of a mate. This biblical absolute will help anyone considering marriage avoid years of heartache: "Be ye not unequally yoked" (2 Corinthians 6:14).

You can be "unequally yoked" in a variety of ways. Small may marry tall. Ignorant may marry intellectual. Old may marry young. Baptist may marry Episcopal. Irish may marry French. Brown may marry yellow. Rich may marry poor. The combinations are many.

Only *one* combination, however, is sin—believer marrying unbeliever. This must be a conviction. All other combinations may meet the frown or smile of society's convention or rules. Culture and customs however, do not carry the same weight as the commands given in Scripture. If you choose to violate God's guidelines, the consequences can have eternal repercussions.

"Be ye not unequally yoked together with unbelievers: for what fellowship hath righteousness with unrighteousness? and what communion hath light with darkness? And what concord hath Christ with Belial? or what part hath he that believeth with an infidel? And what agreement hath the temple of God with idols? For ye are the temple of the living God; as God hath said, I will dwell in them, and walk in them; and I will be their God, and they shall be my people. Wherefore come out from among them, and be ye separate, saith the Lord, and touch not the unclean thing; and I will receive you" (2 Corinthians 6:14-17).

This statement is not the rule of a denomination. It is the Word of God. To do contrary is to violate your conscience.

When The Yoke Isn't Equal

The book of Job provides an example of an "unequally yoked" marriage. This man, Job, who was "perfect and upright, and one that feared God, and eschewed evil" (Job 1:1), was married to an ungodly woman.

When Job lost all his possessions, his children, and his health, his wife's response was anything but spiritual. "Then said his wife unto him, Dost thou still retain thine integrity? Curse God, and die" (Job 2:9). If there was ever a time when Job needed his wife's comfort and strength, it was at the moment she let him down.

How did Job handle the situation? "But he said unto her, Thou speakest as one of the foolish women speaketh. What? Shall we receive good at the hand of God, and shall we not receive evil? In all this did not Job sin with his lips" (Job 2:10). Job did not accuse his wife of any violation of the marital contract. He simply tagged her "foolish."

Satan had been given permission to attack God's servant, Job, on a wide front—barred only from taking his life. Was Mrs. Job one of the weapons Satan used against her husband?

Maybe Job was too soft or too hen-pecked to stand up to his wife's sarcasm and belligerency. It's possible he had long before submitted to this matrimonial trial, seeing his wife as a feminine "thorn in his flesh."

"Shall I not receive evil?" he said. Does this mean that all marital unhappiness, spiritual mismatches in wedlock, and unsympathetic mates are from "the hand of God"?

What should a godly, righteous man do in such a situation? Is it all right to divorce a woman who is not on the same spiritual level as you are? King David may have thought so! His wife, Michal, was embarrassed by her husband's enthusiastic expression of worship.

"Michal daughter of Saul watched from a window. When she saw king David leaping and dancing before the Lord, she despised him in her heart. . . ." When David returned home to bless his household, Michal came out to meet him and said, 'How the king of Israel has distinguished himself today, disrobing in the sight of the slave girls of his servants as any vulgar fellow would!' " (2 Samuel 6:16,20 *NIV*).

Michal's jealous words brought a sharp rebuke from her husband, who in essence replied, "If you don't like it, you can lump it!"

"David said to Michal, 'It was before the Lord, who chose me rather than your father or anyone from his house when he appointed me ruler over the Lord's people Israel—I will celebrate before the Lord' " (verse 21 *NIV*).

After that episode, their marriage was never the same. "Therefore Michal the daughter of Saul had no child unto the day of her death" (2 Samuel 6:23).

The relationship between Michal and David had not always been so strained. Early in their marriage she risked her own life to save his. "And Michal Saul's daughter loved David" (1 Samuel 18:20). Some couples can commune sexually, be physically attracted, yet be a gulf apart spiritually.

What would the apostle Paul advise? First, and emphatically, he would say, "Look before you leap." But if the alliance is formed, what then? "If any brother have a wife that believeth not, and she be pleased to dwell with him, let him not put her away" (1 Corinthians 7:13).

The believer is to make the best of the situation— like Job did. An attitude of humility can produce Christlike character and may result in the salvation of the unbelieving partner.

Your marriage may be less than the ideal. You may even be unequally yoked to an unbeliever. But no matter what your situation, you are responsible before God to fulfill the conditions of your contract—to love, honor, and cherish. Such a tremendous task can only be accomplished with supernatural help. Only God, by His Holy Spirit, can take two distinct personalities and weave them into *one*.

The apostle Paul describes the kind of love-relationship that fulfills God's original design for marriage: "Fulfil ye my joy, that ye be likeminded, having the same love, being of one accord, of one mind" (Philippians 2:2). In the next few chapters, we will look at some practical ways you and your spouse can develop this kind of oneness in your marriage.

25. Husbands, love your wives, even as Christ also loved the church, and gave himself for it;

26. That he might sanctify and, cleanse it with the washing of water by the word,

27. That he might present it to himself a glorious church, not having spot, or wrinkle, or any such thing; but that it should be holy and without blemish.

28. So ought men to love their wives as their own bodies. He that loveth his wife loveth himself.

29. For no man ever yet hated his own flesh; but nourisheth and cherisheth it, even as the Lord the church:

30. For we are members of his body, of his flesh, and of his bones.

31. For this cause shall a man leave his father and mother, and shall be joined unto his wife, and they two shall be one flesh.

3

FALLING & RISING IN LOVE

An old Hebrew proverb says, "You don't *fall* in love—you *rise* in love." Falling in love is a wonderful, romantic feeling, but it takes more than feeling to maintain a marriage.

"Set me as a seal upon thine heart, as a seal upon thine arm: for love is strong as death. . . . Many waters cannot quench love, neither can the floods drown it" (Song of Solomon 8:6,7).

In this passage, a woman asks to have her name or likeness stamped upon her lover's heart and arm—on his breast above his heart as a seat of affection, and on his arm where it would be constantly in view. Every woman longs to be kept in tender remembrance by the man she loves.

In order to survive, love must have love in return. Nothing is as devastating as unrequited love. When a woman feels, "I cannot reach him, no matter how hard I try," turmoil and frustration eventually break her heart.

The woman in Solomon's Song fears that love may be diminished by distance. She trembles at the thought of "out of sight, out of mind." Love reaches for reminders—pictures, letters, vows, or exchanges. The lover cries out for a "seal"—a ring, a locket, or something close to the heart that will say, "I am his and he is mine."

When the woman asks her lover to set her "as a seal" upon his arm, she is asking for protection. The arm is a symbol of strength and power. When a woman reaches for the arm of a man, she is publicly saying, "Defend me! Escort me! See me through!"

This young woman was not satisfied with an agreement giving her all the strength of Solomon's kingdom. Although material wealth would satisfy an ambitious adventuress, it could never satisfy a sincerely loving heart. A true companion says, "I don't want things. I want *you*." "Set me as a seal upon thine heart."

This is the secret of a good marriage. As long as each partner is in the other's heart, love will sustain the marriage. "Love is strong!" It will survive the trials and tribulations that come to every home. "Many waters cannot quench love, neither can the floods drown it." The sustaining power of love is the greatest force known to mankind.

A Love Story

Everyone enjoys a good love story, and the romances of the Old Testament are unparalled in historical literature—Abraham and Sarah, Isaac and Rebekah, Jacob and Rachel.

Even Romeo and Juliet can't compare to Isaac and Rebekah's romantic encounter. For them it was love at first sight. Like a line from the great musical, *South Pacific*—"Across the room . . . ," it happened.

The book of Genesis describes their first encounter: "And Isaac went out to meditate in the field at the eventide: and he lifted up his eyes, and saw, and, behold, the camels were coming. And Rebekah lifted up her eyes, and when she saw Isaac, she lighted off the camel. For she had said unto the servant, What man is this that walketh in the field to meet us? And the servant had said, It is my master: therefore she took a veil, and covered herself" (Genesis 24:63-65).

What was Isaac doing walking in the field? What were his thoughts out there in the Negev at sunset? Isaac was a lonely, pensive man. His mother, Sarah, had died, and he needed greater comfort than the fields and his father's wealth could supply.

In that moment of frustration, Isaac "looked up."

But he saw more than camels. Isaac's eyes fell upon a scene that could, and did, erase all his loneliness and quest for peace.

We are not told what happened from the moment Rebekah saw Isaac until we read: "Isaac brought her into his mother Sarah's tent and took Rebekah, and she became his wife; and he loved her: and Isaac was comforted after his mother's death" (Genesis 24:67). What a warm and exciting evening that must have been!

The writer of Proverbs says, "Let thy fountain be blessed: and rejoice with the wife of thy youth. Let her be as the loving hind and pleasant roe; let her breasts satisfy thee at all times; and be thou ravished always with her love" (Proverbs 5:18-19). Only in marriage can we experience such magnificent dimensions of pleasure and joy.

Although Isaac and Rebekah's romance certainly included the sexual dimension, their relationship went far beyond physical pleasure. A finer, more delicate texture can be felt in this marriage. Their intimate devotion to one another combined the joy of sharing common goals with an unswerving purpose to fulfill God's will.

There is more to marriage than sex, but Hollywood and Broadway's warped formula of "love" seldom goes beyond the bedroom. The finer ingredients of mutuality and responsibility are excluded from the screen's version of romance. Yet, without these deeper qualities, sex cannot hold a marriage together.

Many times the Bible uses the word "know" to describe the intimate, physical relationship between a man and a woman. In the case of Isaac and Rebekah, however, another word is used: Isaac "loved" her (Genesis 24:67). A permanent and enduring partnership is built on the second word, *love*, not on the first, *know*.

The root meaning of love is "to give." In this sense, Isaac was a true lover. He knew how to take and draw comfort from Rebekah's love, but he also knew how to be at her side and give her strength when she needed it. During a difficult time in their marriage, Isaac stood by his wife in prayer:

"Isaac intreated the Lord for his wife, because she was barren: and the Lord was intreated of him, and Rebekah his wife conceived" (Genesis 25:21). What an excellent example of the fact that "the effectual fervent prayer of a righteous man availeth much" (James 5:16).

Too many husbands make widows of their wives in spiritual things. While she goes to prayer meeting, he spends the evening at the bowling alley. This, however, was not the case with Isaac and Rebekah. They were true partners.

Isaac and Rebekah not only knew how to *pray* together; they knew how to *play* together. We are told: "Abimelich king of the Philistines looked out at a window, and saw, and behold Isaac was sporting with Rebekah his wife" (Genesis 26:8).

This couple found their ultimate pleasure and relaxation in delighting one another—this is romance at its best! No one else could compete for Isaac's affections, and Rebekah made sure no Hagar or Leah or Bathsheba would ever invade her marriage. She was Isaac's one-and-only.

Love, in the case of Isaac and Rebekah, was *instantaneous,* but it was also *continuous.* The sustaining power of love transcends feeling and develops into a mature, lasting relationship.

Rising To The Challenge

Every creature in the animal kingdom faces predators who are their natural enemies. In times of danger, an animal must use his God-given defenses against his attacker or be devoured. Marriage, too, has a natural enemy—an adversary who prowls about, "seeking whom he may devour" (1 Peter 5:8).

As the head of the marriage relationship, the believer-husband must be on the alert. It is his duty to use all the weapons of faith to defend and protect his marital relationship. *Love* is the defensive weapon that will ward off the enemy's attacks. "Nevertheless let every one of you in particular so love his wife even as himself" (Ephesians 5:33).

Cultivating love is the believer-husband's responsibility. Marriage is like a garden that must be constantly nourished with affection, attention, and tender loving care. "Ye husbands, dwell with them according to knowledge, giving honour unto the wife, as unto the weaker vessel, and as being heirs together of the grace of life" (1 Peter 3:7).

The most difficult relationship entrusted to man is the one he has with his wife. Maintaining a happy marriage demands brave and determined men who will rise to the challenge the way mountain climbers face Mt. Everest and astronauts shoot for the moon. This is no job for sissies!

"Husbands, love your wives, even as Christ also loved the church, and gave himself for it" (Ephesians 5:25). This command is more easily preached than practiced and requires great determination and initiative on the husband's part. Even the best among us must work at it.

How can I maintain what I felt for my wife before I signed the marriage contract? This is the task before me and every husband. Using Jesus as our example, I want to share ten ways Christian husbands can and should show love to their wives.

1. *You love by service.*

"By love serve one another" (Galatians 5:13). You can manifest love in many ways—vacuum the carpet, clear the table, babysit for an evening. Jesus came not to be ministered unto but to minister. He had a servant's heart—He washed His disciples feet. Have you ever washed your wife's back or massaged her legs?

Put yourself in your wife's position and see things from her point of view. Imagine what it's like to be at home all day with the children. Ask yourself, "How can I best share and lift my wife's burden?" When this attitude becomes the working principle in your relationship, happiness is sure to follow.

Actions speak louder than words. Exalt her as "first lady" of your kingdom! See that she is served first at the table before the children or an important guest. Bring her breakfast in bed and let her feel like Miss America or Queen-for-a-Day.

2. *You love by the unusual.*

Jesus is always full of surprises. He goes beyond maintaining the status quo to "life more abundantly." If you use Jesus as your example, your wife will think she's married to Mr. Excitement! Love will find and arrange surprises. An unexpected supper date or a small gift like a piece of jewelry maintains the element of suspense and mystery in your relationship.

Court your wife! Repeat the honeymoon. Emboss it with a night away from home complete with an elegant suite and proper service. Provide that "season of refreshing" for your marriage. Every woman needs a mountain-top experience periodically. Only then can she descend to household chores and the demands of dirty clothes, dusty furniture, and crying babies.

Love is going the extra mile as well as turning the other cheek. Lift your wife out of the crush and weariness of her burdensome schedule. Relieve her from something she feels must be done. Routines and the usual become boring and irksome. Sweep her off her feet, and foster the love of adventure in her soul.

3. *You love when you remember.*

Jesus knew the importance of celebrating special occasions—"This do in remembrance" (1 Corinthians 11:24). Remember your wife's birthday, Valentine's Day, your wedding anniversary! Nothing assassinates a marriage faster than ignoring events that are precious to her. Forgetting cannot be excused. Make it your business to remember special days—don't force her to remind you.

Those little investments in love—the phone call from work, the flowers, the fulfillment of an anticipated surprise, the special card—cost so little and mean so much. Over the years I have learned that long after a gift has surpassed its usefulness, the card accompanying the gift is kept and treasured. Women store sentiments. Now I buy less expensive gifts and more expensive cards. Remembering special dates on the calendar keeps the joy in your marriage and guarantees your wife's contentment.

4. *You love when you pay attention to your wife.*
The good advice of a well-known television commercial, "Reach out and touch someone," can be taken to heart. Any husband would be wise to reach out and take the hand of his wife or gently hug her shoulders whenever he has the opportunity. Another expression, taken from an old song, "Have I Told You Lately That I Love You?" will effectively convey your affection and let your wife know you care.

Your wife needs to see your promise "to cherish" activated and practiced in daily living. Present her with a gift certificate or leave a little note on her dressing-table before you leave for work. Whenever you go out together, open doors for her and graciously seat her at the table. Be sure to introduce her to your friends and include her in your conversation.

By paying attention to your wife in the little areas of life, you can avoid many of the deep pitfalls in marriage. Be the first one to compliment your wife on her appearance—before some other man does. If you fall into the habit of unawareness, your wife will soon suspect, "I don't think he even realizes that I am around." Nothing is as deadly as the habit of taking her for granted.

Jesus is always aware of His sheep. "I am the good shepherd, and know my sheep, and am known of mine" (John 10:14). You show your wife that you care by being aware of her and her need for attention.

5. *You love when you communicate with your wife.*

Your wife needs to know that your marriage relationship with her is the most important area of your life. One way to do this is to share things with her that cannot be shared with anyone else. Make your wife your confidante. Let her be the safe-deposit box of your secrets and ambitions. Don't alienate her with a superior attitude or keep things to yourself because you think she won't understand. Your wife should be your best friend.

Keep your conversations fresh and interesting.

Dissect everything that happens at the office or in the kitchen. Experiences are delightful. Learn to listen and explore them together. Your wife's world is probably more exciting than you think— maybe even more so than yours!

Loving always *costs* something. Give of yourself to your wife. Make a special effort to find time to be alone with her. Serenade your spouse with long-playing albums of love songs from your courting days. Find phrases that express what you feel and don't be afraid to let your convictions surface. I love to repeat to my wife the words that Jim Nabors so magnificently sings on one of his most popular records, "With you by my side, tomorrow never comes!"

Jesus unashamedly loved His own: "Love one another, as I have loved you. Greater love hath no man than this, that a man lay down his life for his friends" (John 15:12-13).

6. *You love when you try to please your wife.*
Too many husbands confine pleasure to what pleases them. "Let every one of us please his neighbor . . . for even Christ pleased not himself" (Romans 15:2,3). Your wife certainly deserves more consideration than a neighbor.

Instead of spending the afternoon watching a ballgame on TV, take her shopping or to the ballet. By showing interest in her hobbies and activities, you build her self-esteem and increase her pleasure.

If she enjoys having her hair done once a week, indulge her. Be generous when it comes to pleasing your wife. In fact, encourage her to get a facial and a manicure, too. Let her enjoy feeling beautiful, and you'll reap the benefits of an attractive and contented wife.

7. *You love when you fill her life with beauty.*
The world is full of dust, dirt, and garbage. Life abounds with endless labor, disappointment, and sorrow. To offset the ugliness of living in a fallen world, fill her life with beauty. Shower her days with flowers, lovely clothes, and perfumes. Soften her nights with candles, music, and fluffy pillows. She needs "paradise regained" now.

If she wants to remodel the kitchen or refurbish the living room, don't make her feel guilty about improving her environment. Her house is her world, and the more attractive and pleasant she can make it, the happier she'll be at home.

Love grows in a garden and bears a scent that arouses the best in us. For instruction on how to treat your wife, Christian husband, read the Song of Solomon, and your marriage will never be the same.

8. *You love when you reflect yourself in your wife.*

Jesus loves the Church and wants us to show forth His character and victory in our lives. This is also true in the husband/wife relationship.

Your wife is a reflection of you and your affection for her. When other people look at your spouse, they see your level of success and your degree of affection. Latin men, especially Italians, dress their wives in a way that says to their competition, "Look, Tony, see how well I am doing!"

A wife who appears bedraggled says to others that her husband is cheap and selfish. As her provider, it is your responsibility to see that your wife reflects you to the best possible advantage at all times.

You are also a reflection of your wife, and she wants to be proud of you. The way you handle yourself in public can either edify her or embarrass her. Nothing humiliates a woman like her husband's bumbling awkwardness in social situations. Be a diplomat and learn to handle relationships skillfully. Jesus always knew what to say and do, even in the most demanding circumstances.

9. *You love when you appreciate your wife.*

Love is a constant sense of appreciation that generates a flow of response: "Thank you for ironing my shirts." "Thank you for a tidy home." "Thank you for looking nice for me." Fill your wife's days with praise and compliments that express how much you appreciate her.

Be happy in her presence. Whistle a merry tune! Hum a love melody. Let your *joy* be known. In the morning, greet her rising with music and not with mutterings. Fill her days with sunshine, and tuck her in at night with delight.

"Rejoice evermore. . . . In everything give thanks: for this is the will of God in Christ Jesus concerning you" (2 Thessalonians 5:16,18). If you love, you are contagious with gratitude and appreciation.

10. *You love when you provide security for your wife.*

Do your best to provide for your wife's needs. A husband who spends all the available cash on his own pleasures while his wife goes to church in run-down high heels and a ragged coat is selfish. Nothing degrades a wife more than having to beg for a few dollars. If a husband doesn't trust his wife with money, he will destroy her self-esteem and make her feel worthless.

Keep your wife informed of the financial condition of the household. When she knows exactly what there is to make ends meet, she will make it stretch farther. Women are born shoppers and generally good money managers. By keeping her up-to-date on your insurance policies, investments, and banking procedures, you are expressing confidence in her managerial abilities. If you are taken by death or incapacitated by accident, your wife will not find herself unprepared to manage legally and financially.

Look to the future and make preparations for your wife's financial security after your retirement or death. Don't leave her with a pile of debts after you're gone. Before His death, Jesus planned and provided for our needs. "Let not your hearts be troubled ... I go to prepare a place for you" (John 14:1-2). Love protects and prepares for the future.

More Than Romance

When you and your wife stood before the pastor and recited your marriage vows, you made many promises: "I take this woman to be my wedded wife, to live with her after God's ordinance in the holy estate of matrimony—to love, honor, and keep her in sickness and in health, and forsaking all others—keeping only unto her so long as we both shall live."

Love is more than romance. It is actively showing you care for your wife in tangible, practical ways. Now that you've fallen in love, rise to the challenge of making your marriage a happy one.

Love your wife the way Isaac loved Rebekah—the way Jesus loves His Bride, the Church.

1. *Though I speak with the tongues of men and of angels, and have not charity, I am become as sounding brass, or a tinkling cymbal.*

2. *And though I have the gift of prophecy, and understand all mysteries, and all knowledge; and though I have all faith, so that I could remove mountains, and have not charity, I am nothing.*

3. *And though I bestow all my goods to feed the poor, and though I give my body to be burned, and have not charity, it profiteth me nothing.*

4. *Charity suffereth long, and is kind; charity envieth not; charity vaunteth not itself, is not puffed up,*

5. *Doth not behave itself unseemly, seeketh not her own, is not easily provoked, thinketh no evil;*

6. *Rejoiceth not in iniquity, but rejoiceth in the truth;*

7. *Beareth all things, believeth all things, hopeth all things, endureth all things.*

4
MARRIAGE-SUCCESS FORMULA

Throughout our marriage, I have always known that Dorothy is in my corner. When I step onto the stage or platform to speak, my first move is to find her in the audience.

Dorothy loves to sit incognito at a convention and hear what people in their seats are saying about me. Later, back in the hotel room, my wife tells me the truth. This can be a humbling experience, but I appreciate her honesty. She helps keep me in line. "No man should think more highly of himself than he ought to think."

Yet, Dorothy is always the first to say, "That was a marvelous message!" When a man hears that from his side-kick, he can "run through a troop and leap over a wall."

I often tell husbands, "Seek God's guidance on Sunday and listen to your wife Monday through Saturday, and you will seldom go wrong."

Dr. Robert Schuller, pastor of the Crystal

Cathedral in Anaheim, California, says his wife gives him signals from her seat in the congregation. If he is speaking too loudly, she will place a finger in her ear. If he is not speaking loudly enough, she will cup an ear with her hand. "But there are times," Dr. Schuller says, "when she will pinch her nose with her fingers." That's when he knows he had better get to the point and wind things up.

Most wives are unaware of the power they hold in their hands and on their lips. With a word, a wife can build up or tear down the self-esteem that has taken her husband years to develop.

With this awesome power comes great responsibility. Let's look back in the Old Testament to see how one woman used her beauty and influence to change her nation.

The Outward Appearance

In the book of Esther, the characters of two beautiful women are recorded: Vashti and Esther. The first, after a brief mention, faded into obscurity. Esther, however, became famous and changed the course of history.

The Bible tells how, in a single day, Queen Vashti's life dramatically changed: "Vashti the queen made a feast for the women in the royal house which belonged to King Ahasuerus. On the seventh day, when the heart of the king was merry with wine, he commanded Mehuman. . . to bring Vashti the queen before the king with the crown royal, to shew the people and the princes her beauty; for she was fair to look upon. But the queen Vashti refused to come at the king's commandment by his chamberlains: therefore was the king very wroth, and his anger burned in him" (Esther 1:9-12).

Queen Vashti's refusal to be gawked at led to her dismissal and expulsion. Her behavior was ruled as contempt, an offense violating the dignity of the king.

As a young woman bred in the ways of Jehovah, Esther filled the gap and stepped into Vashti's place. "And the king loved Esther above all the women, and she obtained grace and favour in his sight more than all the virgins; so that he set the royal crown upon her head, and made her queen instead of Vashti" (Esther 2:17).

Esther was a beauty, no doubt about it. But, unlike Vashti, Esther knew how to use her appearance and charm in positive ways. Although she was no less opposed to ungodliness and male chauvinism than was Vashti, Esther had an advantage the former queen didn't have—she had God on her side.

During the crisis that threatened the lives of her people, Esther took her own life in her hands by requesting an audience with her husband. She needed a favorable response from the king—anything less could be fatal to herself and others.

Esther combined *natural* appeal with *spiritual* urgency. She carefully selected apparel to catch the king's eye while at the same time requesting the prayer support of her maidens. Although this great queen knew the place of intercession, she was also aware of the selling power of physical attraction. Her wisdom may have come from the prophet who said, "Man looketh on the outward appearance . . . the Lord looketh on the heart" (1 Samuel 16:7).

To enhance her "outward appearance," Queen Esther "put on her royal apparel" (Esther 5:1). She gave God something to bless. All the resources the Creator and nature provided were used by the queen to produce allurement. And it worked!

"When the king saw Esther the queen standing in the court . . . she obtained favour in his sight: and the king held out to Esther the golden sceptre that was in his hand. So Esther drew near" (Esther 5:2).

Sparkling With Appeal

Enhancing beauty with cosmetics and jewelry sharpens and highlights a woman's natural assets. When a woman wears something precious, she transmits the feeling of being precious herself. A healthy marriage relationship requires sparkle and appeal. The bride who "adorneth herself with her jewels" (Isaiah 61:10) is often mentioned in the Bible. Many brides, however, quickly slide from bride status to bore status.

Some "religious" women take pride in wearing ill-fitting, frumpy clothes guaranteed to make them unattractive. Because they have been taught that wearing makeup is sinful, they think a pale, blotchy complexion is an advertisement for consecration.

It is never unspiritual for a godly woman to make herself as attractive as possible. "Your body is the temple of the Holy Ghost ... therefore glorify God in your body, and in your spirit, which are God's" (1 Corinthians 6:19,20).

Flo Zigfield, the famous producer, displayed the most beautiful women he could find for his Zigfield Follies. His wife, Billie, daily faced the fact that these women were competing for her husband's attention. Yet, their marriage of many years was a record for the entertainment industry.

How did Billie survive the competition? Every morning she got up an hour before her husband to make herself as beautiful and ravishing as possible. Mr. Zigfield always awakened to the sight of a well-groomed, attractive wife.

The Lord wants wives to put their natural endowments to the best possible use—for their own good and their husband's pleasure. I believe a wife should dress to please her husband—not the other women in the church. The same goes for hairstyle. A wife should have her hair fixed the way her husband likes it—not in the style preferred by the hairdresser. My wife Dorothy pleases me, and that is what matters.

Secret Ingredients

As a married man, the apostle Peter knew something about husbands and wives. He writes: "Likewise, ye wives, be in subjection to your own husbands; that, if any obey not the word, they also may without the word be won by the conversation [conduct] of the wives" (1 Peter 3:1).

Sometimes a wife must bend a bit toward her husband if she wants to influence or win him for the Lord. In a difficult marital situation, the wife often holds the key to making or breaking the relationship. What kind of conduct must a wife have in order to win her husband and have a happy, successful marriage? According to the apostle Peter, the secret to a wife's success lies in the hidden recesses of a woman's heart—"a meek and quiet spirit" (1 Peter 3:4).

Many women have trouble with the idea of submission. Yet, Scripture clearly states how wives are to behave toward their husbands: "Wives, submit yourselves unto your husbands, as unto the Lord" (Ephesians 5:22). In a successful marriage, submission is not an option—it is a command.

Wives, you'll be surprised what a smile and a gentle spirit can do! A meek and quiet spirit is the most precious and valuable adornment you can put on. In the sight of God, this kind of attitude is of "great price" (1 Peter 3:4).

An old gambler, introduced by a younger gambler to the young man's wife, asked her, "How can you be such a wife to such a husband?"

The sweet wife's lips trembled, and with tears in her eyes, she replied, "My husband is a poor gambler, and I have prayed that God would save him. That hasn't happened, and I know one day my husband will die. So I have determined to make his life as pleasant as possible for him."

Then the old gambler turned on the younger man and said, "How can you be such a husband to such a wife?"

That was enough. The younger man answered, "With God's help I'm going to change my ways. I will surrender to God and try to be a better husband to my wife."

In the book of Galatians, we find a list of special qualities that can make any wife a winner in her marriage. "But the fruit of the Spirit is love, joy, peace, longsuffering, gentleness, goodness, faith, meekness, temperance" (5:22-23).

A wife who possesses these traits in the power of the Holy Spirit has all the ingredients for a successful marriage. Let's look at some of these qualities and how you can put them to work in the relationship with your husband.

Love

The marriage-success formula begins with love. But what is love? The Bible tells us what it is and what it is not: "Love is patient, love is kind. It does not envy, it does not boast, it is not proud. It is not rude, it is not self-seeking, it is not easily angered, it keeps no record of wrongs. Love does not delight in evil but rejoices with the truth. It always protects, always trusts, always hopes, always perseveres" (1 Corinthians 13:4-6, *NIV*).

Saying "I love you" is easy, but putting love into practice in life's daily routines is a far more difficult task. The wife is often the one who has to take more of an initiative in practicing love in the home.

Some husbands are starved for tender, caring affection. In all their years of marriage, they have never known what it means to be loved. I know men who are bound by the fetters of family finance, insurance, property, education, and transportation, but they receive no compensation for their efforts. These husbands feel, "My wife doesn't care for *me*—only for what I can provide."

Women were created with a compassionate and caring nature that reaches out to others. God told Eve, "Thy desire shall be to thy husband" (Genesis 3:16). You will find your greatest satisfaction and fulfillment in loving and caring for the man God has given you.

The bridegroom in the Song of Solomon says, "How fair and how pleasant art thou, O love, for delights!" (7:6). Can your husband say that about you?

Joy

When God created woman, He imagined a helpmate who would sparkle and radiate with joy. "Blessed is the people that know the joyful sound: they shall walk, O Lord, in the light of thy countenance" (Psalm 89:15). A joyful wife has a beautiful countenance.

Elisabeth must have been a joyful wife to her husband, Zacharias, the father of John the Baptist. When her son was born, she filled the parsonage with song. Luke says, "And her neighbours and her cousins heard how the Lord had shewed great mercy upon her; and they rejoiced with her" (Luke 1:58). Joy is contagious.

Gloom is also contagious—like a virus. It multiplies congestion and causes inflammation in the home. If depression and self-pity control your personality, any hope of a happy marriage will elude you.

The secret of a joyful personality is thankfulness. Let your husband know how much you appreciate him for providing for your needs. Gratitude always generates joy that overflows and fills a home with laughter.

Joy communicates strength and nurtures a healthy home environment. Manifest joy in everything you do—in coordinating your outfits and in arranging the centerpiece for your table. When your husband comes home, don't let him find you with unkempt hair, a frown on your face, and dirty dishes in the sink. If your main objective in marriage is to make life pleasant for your husband, he will never look beyond the joy of his homelife for fulfillment.

Peace

If you determine to make your home a happy one, peace will also reign there. Show me a wife who is a peacemaker, and I'll show you a winner. "Blessed are the peacemakers: for they shall be called the children of God" (Matthew 5:9).

A woman with an argumentative spirit makes life miserable for her husband. "It is better to dwell in a corner of the housetop, than with a brawling woman in a wide house" (Proverbs 21:9).

True inner peace can only be obtained by trusting in the Lord. "Thou wilt keep him in perfect peace, whose mind is stayed on thee: because he trusteth in thee" (Isaiah 26:3). Learn to look to the Lord as your source of security, and your personality will radiate a tranquil assurance that will carry over into your homelife.

During the day find time to spend with the Lord in prayer and Bible study. That is the only way your peace of heart and mind can be maintained. "Be careful [anxious] for nothing; but in every thing by prayer and supplication with thanksgiving let your requests be made known unto God. And the peace of God, which passeth all understanding, shall keep your hearts and minds through Christ Jesus" (Philippians 4:7).

When a man knows he will be greeted at the

door by a contented, peaceful wife, he looks forward to coming home in the evening. Providing your husband with a relaxed, tranquil atmosphere on his arrival from work should be the goal of your day. Housework and children should not be allowed to rob him of a quiet entry into his castle.

Long-Suffering

Another delicious ingredient in the marriage-success formula is long-suffering. This means *to bear and forbear*. If your husband isn't perfect, be patient with him. "Love beareth all things" (1 Corinthians 13:7). Instead of pointing out his faults, help your husband overcome them with encouragement and praise. No one is perfect, and husbands make many blunders—sins of omission and commission.

I love the optimism of our Lord concerning the twelve apostles. These men were quarrelsome, ignorant, ambitious, and unreliable, yet to Jesus they were "the salt of the earth" (Matthew 5:13). It takes a positive attitude to keep on believing in people.

"Forgetting those things which are behind" is an excellent verse to practice in marriage. (See Philippians 3:13.) It's difficult to make any progress if you're always looking back. Saying to your spouse, "I wish I had married him instead of you," destroys any hope for building a lasting relationship. General Douglas McArthur said it well: "When you return to old flames, you usually find ashes."

Long-suffering is one of the greatest attributes of our heavenly Father: "The longsuffering of God waited in the days of Noah, while the ark was preparing, wherein few, that is, eight souls were saved" (1 Peter 3:20). For more than a century, God put up with intolerable, sinful conditions on the earth for the benefit of eight people.

By walking in the Spirit of God, you, too, can develop a long-suffering, patient attitude toward the imperfections and flaws in your husband. Learn to accept him as he is, and allow God to change him into the man He wants him to be.

Gentleness

In our modern American society, gentleness doesn't get too much attention. Instead, women are encouraged to become more assertive and aggressive in the male-dominated working world.

For centuries women have been designated the "gentle sex." That should come as a compliment since the word gentleness implies nobility, consideration, mildness, good breeding, and mannerliness.

When all else fails, you can win with gentleness. Queen Esther did. She faced a vulgar, dangerous situation, but she approached her husband, the king, with humility and grace. "If it seem good unto the king, let the king and Haman come this day unto the banquet that I have prepared for him" (Esther 5:4).

Esther could have given her husband the "either/or" treatment, but she knew that "a soft answer turneth away wrath" and "grievous words stir up anger" (Proverbs 15:1). Gentleness worked for this great queen. "If I have found favour in the sight of the king, and if it please the king . . . ." (Esther 5:8). She did find favor, and her marriage and a nation were saved as a result.

If your marriage is in trouble, try using Esther's method. Approach your husband with gentleness, and you will be surprised at his positive response.

Cultivating Your Garden

God gave Eve a garden and a husband, but Eve allowed an intruder to violate her paradise. If you don't claim your orchard for God, the devil will sow chaos and confusion in your marriage and home.

Your orchard is the fruit of the Spirit—"love, joy, peace, longsuffering, gentleness . . . ." With this kind of fruit growing in your home, the atmosphere will reflect the peace and serenity of the Garden before man's fall.

Without the fruit of the Spirit, you are exposed to the enemy and every kind of trouble he can send your way. Jesus is looking for fruit on the tree of your life. "Behold, these three years I come seeking fruit . . . and find none: cut it down; why cumbereth it the ground?"

Such a statement creates alarm: "Lord, let it alone this year also, till I shall dig about it . . . and if it bear fruit, well: and if not, then after that thou shalt cut it down" (Luke 13:7-9).

Some of you wives have had an inward warning, and you are alarmed. Your fruitless example is an embarrassment to our Lord. Look around you! You have done nothing to improve your marital situation, and the axe is laid at the root of your life. You may be on probation, but the time has come to get to work. This may be your final opportunity.

Don't wait for disaster to strike. Take positive, affirmative action now. Let the Holy Spirit bring good fruit from your life and make you the loving, patient wife God created you to be.

A woman's ways are God's gift to the feminine gender. Learn to use these natural endowments positively in your marriage. Nothing brings greater glory to God than a Christian wife who knows how to love her husband and make him happy. That's the secret to a successful marriage.

10. *Who can find a virtuous woman? for her price is far above rubies.*

11. *The heart of her husband doth safely trust in her, so that he shall have no need of spoil.*

12. *She will do him good and not evil all the days of her life.*

13. *She seeketh wool, and flax, and worketh willingly with her hands.*

14. *She is like the merchants' ships; she bringeth her food from afar.*

15. *She riseth also while it is yet night, and giveth meat to her household, and a portion to her maidens.*

16. *She considereth a field, and buyeth it: with the fruit of her hands she planteth a vineyard.*

17. *She girdeth her loins with strength, and strengtheneth her arms.*

18. *She perceiveth that her merchandise is good: her candle goeth not out by night.*

19. *She layeth her hands to the spindle, and her hands hold the distaff.*

20. *She stretcheth out her hand to the poor; yea, she reacheth forth her hands to the needy.*

21. She is not afraid of the snow for her household: for all her household are clothed with scarlet.

22. She maketh herself coverings of tapestry; her clothing is silk and purple.

23. Her husband is known in the gates, when he sitteth among the elders of the land.

24. She maketh fine linen, and selleth it; and delivereth girdles unto the merchant.

25. Strength and honour are her clothing; and she shall rejoice in time to come.

26. She openeth her mouth with wisdom; and in her tongue is the law of kindness.

27. She looketh well to the ways of her household, and eateth not the bread of idleness.

28. Her children arise up, and call her blessed; her husband also, and he praiseth her.

29. Many daughters have done virtuously, but thou excellest them all.

30. Favour is deceitful, and beauty is vain: but a woman that feareth the Lord, she shall be praised.

5

THE PERFECT WIFE

Whenever we see the word "perfect," our first impulse is to cringe and reply, "No one is perfect!" But perfection is God's ideal, and He sets forth high standards in His Word, the Bible—not to condemn us but to give us something to shoot for.

The thirty-first chapter of Proverbs provides a picture of ideal womanhood according to God's standard. In detail, the attributes of a God-fearing, hard-working, kind and virtuous wife are described. As we study these qualities, let God's Word challenge you to strive to become the kind of woman He wants you to be.

1. *The ideal woman is virtuous.*

Verse ten of chapter thirty-one says, "Who can find a virtuous woman? for her price is far above rubies." Finding a woman of high character must have been difficult in Solomon's days because she is compared to such a precious stone.

A virtuous woman has her heart right before the Lord, and her lifestyle reflects an unwavering obedience to God's Word. A wife like that is certainly of great benefit to her husband. In fact, the Bible says, "A virtuous woman is a crown to her husband" (Proverbs 12:4).

When we think of a "crown," we visualize a beautiful, golden ornament glittering with costly jewels. In the same way, a virtuous wife adds beauty and sparkle to her husband's life. As an object of great value, a crown is cherished and protected by its owner. Any husband who has a virtuous wife will do everything in his power to cherish and protect his most precious possession. Being a virtuous woman certainly has its rewards—for both husband and wife.

2. The ideal woman is dependable.

This attribute of dependability is most evident in the wife's relationship with her husband. "The heart of her husband doth safely trust in her, so that he shall have no need of spoil" (Proverbs 31:11). He has full confidence in his wife's love and respect for him, and all his needs are met.

In her quiet, efficient way the ideal wife lets her husband know he is worthwhile and that she couldn't get along without him. When he comes home, she refreshes him morally, emotionally, physically, and mentally. The next morning she sends him back to his job encouraged and built up. As long as a man feels loved and appreciated at home, he can put up with almost anything at work.

When a man loses his job or has some other financial setback, he needs his wife's support more than ever. A loving wife furnishes the "reserve" her husband requires in tough times. She stands in his corner, cheering him on.

Bill Klem, dean of all major league umpires, once told a young, prospective umpire that he should be married. "When it seems all the world is against you—when fans boo and players criticize," he told the newcomer, "that's the time you need someone to love you and tell your troubles to."

When your husband needs you, be there for him. Assist him in any way you can, without nagging or complaining about the situation. A husband can trust a dependable wife because he knows she always has his best interests at heart.

"Let . . . the wife see that she reverence her husband" (Ephesians 5:33). If your mate knows you respect him, he will have the assurance and confidence to be all God wants him to be. Happy is the man who receives encouragement and inspiration from his wife to *do* his best and *be* his best.

3. *The ideal wife is an asset to her husband.*

"She will do him good and not evil all the days of her life" (Proverbs 31:12). This is the ideal wife's main objective in her marriage—to do her husband good. Her steady, unwavering devotion gives him strength to face the world with courage.

In public he doesn't have to worry about what she will say about him or how she will act. A wife who wants to make her husband look good doesn't jump in with the punchline when he is telling a story. She never discounts him publicly by saying, "Oh, you never tell it right!" Instead she builds him up and always protects him from ridicule.

The husband of the Proverbs woman is "known in the gates, when he sitteth among the elders of the land" (verse 23). How do you think he reached such a high position of prestige and authority in his community? His wife encouraged him, always telling him he could do better. She listened to his ideas, supported his opinions, and helped him reach his goals.

A well-known sales-and-marketing consultant made this rather revealing statement: "I have never known a totally competent man who succeeded without the belief and admiration of a woman behind him." That conclusion supports the often-expressed conviction that "behind every successful man is a great woman." If you help your husband reach his full potential, you will be the main recipient of his success.

Some wives, however, are more of a hindrance than a help to their husbands' careers. Jezebel, as the Bible records, was a hindrance. "There was none like Ahab, which did sell himself to work wickedness in the sight of the Lord, whom Jezebel his wife stirred up" (1 Kings 21:24). Ahab's wife blunted every decent impulse this man ever had, and she made a mockery out of his title, "king of Israel."

The wife of Louis Pasteur, the great scientist, resolved from the first days of their marrige that "the laboratory must come before everything." She kept her vow. On their thirty-fifth wedding anniversary, she wrote to one of their children, "Your father is absorbed in his thoughts, talks little, sleeps little, rises at dawn, and in one word continues the life I began with him this day thirty-five years ago."

Mrs. Pasteur's unwavering support of her husband and his goals enabled this gifted man to fight disease and make medical history. Many lives have been saved as a result of his valuable discoveries. Your husband's success or failure in life may lie in your hands.

4. *The ideal woman is a good homemaker.*

"She seeketh wool, and flax, and worketh willingly with her hands. She is like the merchants' ships; she bringeth her food from afar. She riseth also while it is yet night, and giveth meat to her household, and a portion to her maidens" (Proverbs 31:13-15).

A wife has many roles—cook, housekeeper, accountant, purchaser, mother, counselor, chauffeur, interior decorator, gardener, etc. This fulltime job requires a capable, well-rounded individual who keeps herself informed and up-to-date. "Every wise woman buildeth her house" (Proverbs 14:1).

Remember the poem of yesteryear, "It takes a heap of living to make a house a home"? A home is more than a fancy condominium or an expensive country club estate. Many of today's brides do not have the foggiest idea how to make a home because they have never been taught. Their lives have been a hodge-podge of baby-sitters, undisciplined classrooms, fastfood restaurants, television, and rock music.

Young brides often bring little more than their bodies to their wedding day. But it takes far more than a physical relationship to build a happy home and a successful marriage. Queen Esther's success depended on her skills in the areas of cooking, hospitality, conversation, intelligence, spirituality, good manners, charm, grace, and courage.

Can you manage a home? Are you capable of dealing with sickness, unemployment, and adversity? Can you cook and sew? Do you read? Can you make intelligent conversation? Do you pray for your husband and your children?

The virtuous woman described in Proverbs 31 "looketh well to the ways of her household, and eateth not the bread of idleness" (verse 27). Being a housewife is no job for the lazy and undisciplined woman. Making a house a home takes constant maintainance and perseverance, but the rewards are a happy husband and a contented family.

5. *The ideal wife is a good money manager.*

"She considereth a field, and buyeth it: with the fruit of her hands she planteth a vineyard. . . . She perceiveth that her merchandise is good: her candle goeth not out by night. She layeth her hands to the spindle, and her hands hold the distaff. . . . She is not afraid of the snow for her household: for all her household are clothed with scarlet. . . . She maketh fine linen, and selleth it; and delivereth girdles unto the merchant" (Proverbs 31:16,18-19,21,24).

This wise and energetic woman knows the value of a dollar and can invest money in profitable ventures. Her God-given talents are put to good use for the family, and she is not afraid of hard work. With her own hands, she plants a garden, makes the children's clothes, and sells her homemade goods for a sizeable profit.

The ideal wife maintains the household budget within the bounds of her husband's paycheck. She doesn't run up bills that cause her husband undue anxiety or create tension in the family. At the same time, she manages to save a few dollars for a rainy day or for that special purchase—like her daughter's graduation dress or her son's soccer shoes.

6. *The ideal woman is unselfish.*

This virtue of selflessness is best characterized by the wife's deeds outside the home. Verse twenty says, "She stretcheth out her hand to the poor; yea, she reacheth forth her hands to the needy." Her world does not revolve around her own selfish pleasures. Reaching beyond the confines of her own household, she seeks to minister to the poor and needy.

A woman who shares with others is easy to live with at home. No one can live happily with a woman who does not know how to give of herself. A wife who is always right or who must always have her own way creates havoc in her homelife. Nothing rocks the matrimonial boat like a demanding wife (or husband, for that matter). Marriage is no place for selfishness.

An unselfish wife makes her husband's interests her interests. She plans a dinner party for his clients and makes sure his suit is pressed for work the next day. After spending all afternoon with Aunt Martha, the selfless wife still finds time to go over tomorrow's math assignment with Johnny. The true test of selflessness is your willingness to go the "second mile."

The story is told about a God-fearing woman who nursed her husband through a long illness. One night, in the wee hours, he awakened to see his wife sitting by his bed—not sewing, not praying—just sitting there. Startled, the husband asked what she was doing. Her reply was: "Nothing, dear! I was just sitting here loving you."

The Proverbs woman found her source of joy and fulfillment in meeting the needs of others. It is no wonder that "her children rise up, and call her blessed; her husband also, and he praiseth her" (Proverbs 31:28).

7. *The ideal wife always looks her best.*
"She maketh herself coverings of tapestry; her

clothing is silk and purple" (Proverbs 31:22). Although the Proverbs woman may make her own clothes, she spares no expense to make sure she looks great.

Italian and Jewish wives always dress in good taste, wearing clothes and jewelry that say, "Joe, or Harry, is doing well." Husbands bask in this kind of quiet publicity. Sarah did it for Abraham. Rebekah did it for Isaac.

The apostle Peter had a lot to say about women and how they are to dress. (See 1 Peter 3:3-5.) His advice probably resulted from his years of personal experience as a married man. (See Luke 4:38.) He knew that true beauty cannot be achieved by wearing gawdy jewelry or flashy clothing. Extremism in any form is vulgar; being *overdressed* is as undesirable as being *underdressed*. The New Testament emphasizes a combination of character and charm. "Whatsoever ye do, do all to the glory of God" (1 Corinthians 10:31).

A wife who always looks her best is an asset to her husband. The fact that the husband of the Proverbs woman is "known in the gates, when he sitteth among the elders of the land" (verse 23) may have something to do with his wife's appearance. Any man running for public office makes sure his wife is on the platform beside him.

Nothing mirrors him to his constituents better than a devoted, attractive wife.

8. *The ideal woman is strong.*

Strength characterizes the woman in Proverbs 31. "She girdeth her loins with strength, and strengtheneth her arms. . . . Strength and honour are her clothing" (verses 17,25). These verses describe a wife who is both physically healthy and emotionally mature.

Nothing so unnerves a man as a whining, complaining wife. Some women are an open invitation for every pharmaceutical commercial and have more headaches than an octopus has arms! A smart wife will guard her health by practicing conservative habits of eating, resting, and exercising—along with New Testament faith.

Many women work hard to keep their homes neat and attractive, while the most important house—their body—is allowed to fall into decay. Remember, your body is not a garage—it is a beautiful temple.

A bride asked her newly acquired husband if he would love her if she grew fat. "No!" he replied. "I promised to stick with you for better or for worse, not through thick or thin!"

The strength talked about in this thirty-first chapter characterizes a dignified, mature woman of faith. The word for "honour" (verse 25) can also be translated "dignity." Proper etiquette and good taste reflect a woman of nobility. Poise and beauty—both physical and spiritual—should be displayed discreetly and effectively.

An attractive woman who does not conduct herself as a lady brings reproach upon herself and her husband. Rudeness of speech and manner are degrading, but "a gracious woman retaineth honour" (Proverbs 11:16).

9. *The ideal woman is cheerful.*

An optimistic, cheerful wife can "rejoice in time to come" (verse 25). No matter how bad things may look, she is never ready to abandon ship. The future doesn't worry this wife because she knows she has prepared for it the best way she can. With her faith in God and confidence in her abilities, she can smile at tomorrow and rest assured that all will be well.

Every little family fuss doesn't become an "armageddon" with her. The ideal wife and mother can spank little Freddie in the morning and laugh at his jokes in the afternoon. She knows that a ready smile and an old-fashioned chuckle are nature's best proven shock-absorbers.

In any marriage, a sense of humor is absolutely necessary. You can't be a missionary, a preacher's wife, a baseball umpire, or even President of the United States without the ability to see the humor in life.

10. *The ideal woman is wise.*

Some people get themselves into trouble every time they open their mouths. But the Proverbs woman "openeth her mouth with wisdom" (verse 26). Literally, this means, "she talks shrewd sense." Neither education nor religion can supply God-given common sense.

Wisdom is the difference between an interesting, entertaining conversationalist and a gossip. It is the difference between a woman who buries herself in lurid, romantic novels and the mother who tells her children a missionary story of courage and faith as she tucks them into bed. "The lips of the wise disperse knowledge: but the heart of the foolish doeth not so" (Proverbs 15:7).

How can a wife and mother properly train her children without faith in God? She will rear pagans otherwise. A godly woman is a nation's greatest asset. The future of our country depends on how far our mothers and our wives pattern their lives after God's ideal of womanhood.

11. *The ideal woman is kind.*

It is written of the godly woman in Proverbs 31

that "in her tongue is the law of kindness" (verse 26). She knew when to speak and how to get her point across in a kind and gracious way.

This world is full of sarcastic and cruel people, and a man doesn't need to face verbal abuse at home after he's encountered it all day at work. The rule of kindness extends to every area of marriage and is the practical outworking of love. Let your words and the way you speak reflect your love for your husband. Love "beareth all things, believeth all things, hopeth all things" (1 Corinthians 13:7-8).

A nagging woman is like a dripping faucet. "A continual dropping in a very rainy day and a contentious woman are alike" (Proverbs 27:15). Both are tormenting and nerve-wracking!

Smart wives never nag. They are diplomats . . . not war secretaries. If the door needs to be repaired, say, "Honey, while I am preparing your favorite meal for dinner, would you please fix the front door?" If that doesn't work, simply suggest hiring someone to make the repairs. That's much better and safer than nagging!

Most of the quarrels in marriage would be eliminated if the husband and wife were as kind and polite to each other as they are to strangers for whom they care very little. Why be rude and cruel to the one you love most? Nothing can cut or leave as deep a scar as a sarcastic word or jibe spoken by a loved one. Make kindness the "law of the land" in your household.

12. *The ideal woman is spiritual.*

In order for a woman to measure up to God's standards, she must be a God-fearing, Christian wife. It doesn't matter how charming or beautiful a woman is, without respect for God she can never be the helpmate God intended. "Favour is deceitful, and beauty is vain: but a woman that feareth the Lord, she shall be praised" (Proverbs 31:30).

A spiritually mature woman has firm convictions based on God's Word and a steadfastness that reflects her commitment. The spokes of a wheel hang loosely if no hub lies at the center. Similarly, life is at loose ends if it is not fastened to faith in Jesus Christ.

Former Governor William E. Russell of Massachusetts tells about the time his boat overturned a mile from shore. He was not a good swimmer, and his friends on shore feared for his life. When he finally reached safety, they asked, "Mr. Russell, how on earth did you ever make it?"

He replied, "I don't know. All I know is I prayed to God and kept my arms and legs working." Mr. Russell learned that faith in God combined with effort on his part saved his life.

Becoming and being an ideal wife and mother also requires both *faith* and *work*. The virtues outlined in Proverbs chapter thirty-one don't come about automatically. You have to work at developing them in your life, and each one is important—dependability, an unselfish spirit, strength, a cheerful attitude, common sense, kindness, and spirituality. As you seek to do and be your best, while trusting God for help, His enabling power will make you more and more the ideal woman He created you to be.

1. *Now concerning the things whereof ye wrote unto me: It is good for a man not to touch a woman.*

2. *Nevertheless, to avoid fornication, let every man have his own wife, and let every woman have her own husband.*

3. *Let the husband render unto the wife due benevolence: and likewise also the wife unto the husband.*

4. *The wife hath not power of her own body, but the husband: and likewise also the husband hath not power of his own body, but the wife.*

5. *Defraud ye not one the other, except it be with consent for a time, that ye may give yourselves to fasting and prayer; and come together again, that Satan tempt you not for your incontinency.*

6

SEX AND THE BELIEVER

God's intention for the marital relationship is stated in this simple command: "Be fruitful and multiply" (Genesis 1:28). The point of debate, however, centers around this question: Is sex intended only for procreation, or is it also intended for health and enjoyment?

Over the centuries the extremists justified this "coming together" for one purpose only—to "multiply." Anything else was considered worldly. Enjoyment and sex appeal were frowned upon. A woman was considered simply a child-bearing machine.

Those who believed sex had an additional purpose—to refurbish, to motivate, to revitalize—were tagged as dangerous. Religious leaders taught that such thinking would be an open invitation to all the devices of Satan.

God never intended for sex to be odious, subversive, or pornographic. Each member of the body is holy by design. No part can say to another, "I have no need of thee" (1 Corinthians 12:21). The grand design is that all parts should be brought into perfect submission and harmony in service pleasing to our heavenly Father.

Nature, the handmaiden of the Creator, is built on the principle of exchange. Male and female sex organs picture the process of recharging. Who would ever consider a flower blossom with its male and female parts *unholy*? Why then do some people think certain organs of the body are blacklisted above others?

The demands of living and working require renewed energy, and sex contributes to our well-being as much as food, drink, and sleep. It is not to be avoided. "Let the husband render unto the wife due benevolence: and likewise also the wife unto the husband" (1 Corinthians 7:3).

The apostle Paul in referring to sex as a "benevolence"—a gift that blesses—lifts it to the spiritual plane. When sex is approached in this way, it becomes a wholesome contribution edifying the entire person.

The Sexual Appetite

In recent years, believers have been liberated from centuries of restrictive mandates imposed

100

on the church. But now a frightening rush toward the other extreme has taken place. The "pill" and other birth-control methods have stimulated sex to a degree of *overdose*. Mankind is reeling from too much.

In the same way a person can indulge in too much salt, too much food, or too much sunshine, too much sex destroys the divine purpose to "be fruitful." Quality is sacrificed for quantity. Instead of being "fruitful," the sexually indulgent become bland, distraught, unbalanced, and jaded. Like any other sensual pleasure, the sexual appetite must be cultured. Too much or too little can be either sickening or strangling.

Teaching in the area of sexual enjoyment is important on every level—at home and in the congregation. "Every one of you should know how to possess his vessel in sanctification and honour" (1 Thessalonians 4:4).

By determining how to implement this command in his or her life, the believer can use sex to make himself or herself "fruitful." This stimulating and rewarding experience is such a personal matter that it cannot be reduced to quotas or formulas.

"But as God hath distributed to every man, as the Lord hath called every one, so let him walk" (1 Corinthians 7:17). I, alone, under God, know what I need and when I need it.

Sex is like hunger or thirst, and I must respect this basic need for sex as a divine impulse. Yet, there is a mannerly and acceptable way to satisfy that need, and it should never fall into the category of the shameful. "And God saw everything that he had made, and, behold, it was very good" (Genesis 1:31).

Cupid's Mighty Arrow

Cupid, that delightful, little angel-character with bow and arrow, derives his name from the ominous-sounding word *concupiscence*. Yet, this old-fashioned, New Testament word has a modern meaning. The Latin verb, *cupere*, means "to desire."

The cupid quality that shoots arrows of desire in us is an asset that must be invested to reap any benefit. Within this area of asset, however, a battle rages. Excitement rises; desire flares; arousal grips; and man burns. Concupiscence is to *desire ardently*. While this meaning includes sexual desire, it also applies to other areas of life.

Saul of Tarsus was a dynamo—a man driven by concupiscence. An eager restlessness created unlimited passion within him. Later, as Paul the apostle, he described the perils of such an adventurous spirit. "But sin, taking occasion [advantage] . . . wrought in me all manner of concupiscence" (Romans 7:8).

For years, Paul had been driven by anger, profanity, sadism, and rebellion. But after his conversion, these powerful drives became a scourge in his life. He tells the Colossians to kill the evil desires lurking within them: "fornication, uncleanness, inordinate affection, evil concupiscence" (Colossians 3:5).

Like all heat, fire, and blaze, ardent desire must be kept under control. Overheating causes damage, so we must know how to possess our vessel "in sanctification and honour; not in the lust of concupiscence, even as the Gentiles which know not God" (1 Thessalonians 4:4,5).

God has loaned me an exciting vehicle for this journey from cradle to coffin. My body has an accelerator, and it has brakes. I am capable of climb, and I can vault into spectacular descent. Varied speeds are at my command, but the course is perilous and demands skill.

Excitement is never to be ruled out. Believer-partners have an obligation to maintain excitement in their physical relationship, but they must learn to keep the fire focused—like a torch. Wrong ideas about "ardent desire" have contributed to the problems facing many Christian couples.

Paul likens the sexual drive to *fire*—"to burn" (1 Corinthians 7:9). This strange element of sex— designed for and allocated to this planet—has engulfed mankind in the flame of sexual passion. Churches and social agencies grapple with this problem of ardent desire gone wild.

How can we regulate these surges of passion? The answers fall into three main categories:

1. Sublimation of the drive
2. Separation from the world
3. Sanctification of the desire

Harnessing The Drive

The driving force within man, the power-plant, focuses its energies, at any given moment, on either the *physical* or *spiritual* aspect of his nature.

Sublimation suggests that I conscript this "physical fire" and harness my energies toward achieving a goal on a higher, spiritual scale. Yielding all my inherent and permissable desires to accomplish a greater, future purpose for God's kingdom brings satisfaction that more than compensates for my sacrifice.

The apostle Paul expects sublimation of married couples when he suggests they can abstain from coming together "that ye may give yourselves to fasting and prayer" (1 Corinthians 7:5).

In sublimation, I simply subordinate my passions. But I am not without reward. I forego my desires so something more valuable may be accomplished.

As my mind and spirit are challenged in other directions, I can augment them by borrowing from my physical energies. The workaholic forces the physical to submit to his demand. By making the "burn" yield to accomplishing his goals, it contributes to his climb up the ladder of success.

One positive outlet for sexual energy is *service*. Be a volunteer! Subliminal satisfaction, as well as physical satisfaction, will result from reading to the infirm, cooking for the church supper, teaching Sunday school, or interceding for the lost. Such service produces blessings that make your sexual expression in marriage of greater value and give it deeper meaning.

Separation From The World

People often seek separation from the world as a means of suppressing their passions. Many men and women have become monks or nuns in an effort to contain their sexual desires.

But is the answer to putting out the fire to become numb? Am I safest in an environment where the law of attraction between the sexes is eliminated? I see nothing that arouses me; I feel nothing that excites me. Hopefully, I will imagine nothing and remember nothing that stimulates my desires. My comfort comes in knowing that others, in company with me, are trying to achieve the same level of numbness.

How long must I ponder whether sex is good or whether it is harmful before the question is settled and I am at spiritual, mental, and physical peace? Maybe a sparse and disciplined diet will help. Perhaps wearing plain, loose, unadorned clothing will speed me toward victory. Maybe if I insolate myself from modern styles, flashing advertisements, worldly entertainment, and the chatter of crowds, I'll be safe.

In the past, restricted religious upbringing created suspicions about all social functions—parties were pitfalls, athletic participation led to compromise, and classical literature was obscene. Anything thought to produce physical excitement was placed out of bounds. Movies were sinful—they were known to breed lust. Popular music was taboo—it could urge toe-tapping and body rhythm. Entertainment, it was thought, was a freeway to sex. Hide! Hide!

During Paul's ministry, a dangerous doctrine was being promoted that forbade marriage. The apostle wrote to Timothy and set the record straight: marriage (along with food) is something "which God hath created to be received with thanksgiving of them which believe and know the truth" (1 Timothy 4:3).

Many brands of separation are preached from the pulpit—regulation of hair and skirt length, degree of cosmetics allowed, acceptable and unacceptable colors of dress. Creeds, disciplines, and regulations have been built to create separation from the world. Putting up fences has become one of the church's favorite pastimes.

Is separation from the world and its temptations the answer to bringing our sexual passions under control? Let's look at the third possible solution before venturing an answer.

Sanctifying The Desire

The final group of answers to the passion problem can be bunched under the heading *sanctification*. What does this mean? The apostle Paul put it this way, "Abstain from all appearance of evil. And the very God of peace sanctify you wholly; and I pray God your whole spirit and soul and body be preserved blameless unto the coming of our Lord Jesus Christ" (1 Thessalonians 5:22-23).

How can I be entirely sanctified? Is it possible for humans to reach such a level of excellence on this side of the grave? Who can withstand ruthless cross-examination and come out smelling like a rose? I believe millions of people would like to be sanctified in this area of sexual desire, but the record is discouraging. Preachers haven't obtained it. What hope can there be for folks in the pew?

Some people argue that if there had been no sex, there would have been no evil in the world. The Bible says, however, "Every man is tempted, when he is drawn away of his own lust, and enticed" (James 1:14).

Sex was not designed as an avenue for carnality. God's intention in creating two sexual beings carried an aura of holiness and total acceptability. "Male and female created he them. . . . And God blessed them. . . . And God saw every thing that he had made, and, behold, it was very good" (Genesis 1:27,28,31). The Creator was obviously very pleased with the arrangement He had made.

Sex was meant to be an avenue of fellowship and pleasure. God's arrangement for this exchange has always been *marriage*. In spite of the assault, ridicule, and analysis of marriage by the world system, man has yet to introduce a better arrangement. If the immorality and adultery trumpeted by the world today is such a hugh success, why are emotional and physical casualties increasing?

Sex enjoys its ultimate fulfillment in an Eden-like environment, not in a ghetto of moral squalor and pig-pen perversion. No wonder Satan has sought to destroy this delightful gift and rob mankind of the joy and beauty of sex in marriage.

"But I say unto you, that whosoever looketh on a woman to lust after her hath committed adultery with her already in his heart" (Matthew 5:28). "Out of the heart proceed evil thoughts, murders, adulteries, fornications, thefts, false witness, blasphemies: These are the things which defile a man" (Matthew 15:19,20). Before sexual passion can be brought under control, the "heart" of an individual must be changed.

"He that soweth to his flesh shall of the flesh reap corruption; but he that soweth to the Spirit shall of the Spirit reap life everlasting" (Galatians 6:8). When the Spirit is in control, our sexual desires cannot corrupt or be corrupted.

Adam and Eve's conjugal relationship in Eden was a pure and holy expression of their love for one another. Although both genders were present—"male and female"—no lust was involved. "And they were both naked, the man and his wife, and were not ashamed" (Genesis 2:25).

Amid the curse of sin in a fallen world, believers must strive to achieve God's design for fruitfulness. Sex is a gift that should be cherished and invested toward abundant life. This special interaction between husband and wife is intended by God to reach into the soul and the spirit. If we as believers recognize and practice the sanctity of sex, our desires will find their fulfillment in His perfect will.

The Act Of Marriage

Many battles are won or lost in the bed! A successful trial attorney in Texas tells women seeking divorce, "How can I win for you in the court what nature's gifts to you have failed to win?"

The writer of Hebrews tells believers, "Marriage is honorable in all, and the bed undefiled" (13:4). Whatever is agreeable and pleasureable to marriage partners is permissable and acceptable. God never considers sex between husband and wife to be "naughty."

A Jewish professor at Yeshiva University says, "A marriage without sexuality is a weak marriage. Every sex act should give maximum pleasure to both parties, and even eroticism has its place, if it does not violate modesty."

Every incentive should be appropriated to make the union between husband and wife "better" and not "worse," "richer" and not "poorer," "healthier" and not "sicker." Sex is God's instrument and should be used to benefit both partners, giving each a sense of fulfillment and belonging. The sexual interchange can make a woman feel beautiful, worthwhile, desirable, confident, and whole. For a man, the act of marriage releases his tensions and reaffirms his masculinity.

Every intimate session is a courtship and demands the same careful preparations that you took on your first night together. *Sensuality* is a female trait while *sexuality* is in the male. One ignites the other. A man's five senses must be awakened by the sight of a lovely body, a delicate scent, an instant response to his touch, the taste of sweet lips, and a voice that urges.

Your days may be filled with activity, but to be a drag at night is disaster for your marriage. Wives should always save some time for their husbands. Nothing deflates a man more than his wife's mundane, "If-you-have-to-I-suppose-you-have-to" attitude.

"Defraud ye not one another" (1 Corinthians 7:5). Probably more fraud is practiced in marriage than in any other area of life. "Not now! I have a headache." "Why don't you think about something

111

else for a change?" "I'm too tired" or "I'm too busy." Marital fraud is an offense.

Don't be a fraud; be a full bed-partner. Paul counseled married couples to "come together again" (1 Corinthians 7:5). This is the secret of marital survival and happiness.

Families where the husband and wife enjoy each other sexually have the happiest homes. But maintaining this special kind of physical enjoyment takes initiative and creativity. Dullness is a sin. A smart woman will keep herself attractive and desirable for her husband, and an intelligent man will give his wife the attention and affection she deserves.

The Male Image

The trend toward a unisex society is becoming stronger and stronger. Is there any reason for us to be concerned? Is gender important to God? "Male and female created he them" (Genesis 1:27). Maybe this is an old-fashioned idea that has lost its relevancy in our modern "tear-down-the-barriers, throw-away-the-mold" society.

God had a purpose in creating two distinct sexes. "It is not good that the man should be alone; I will make him an help meet for him" (Genesis 2:18). The emphasis in this verse is on "help." Although God placed Adam in a paradise, He knew that man needed fellowship on a human level.

"And God said, Let us make man in our image, after our likeness" (Genesis 1:26). The male by the decision of the Creator has a designated role. He is to be priest of the household and defender of his family. To deface or try to erase this image—to reduce the male to a lesser stature— is to upset God's original design and purpose for man.

The world wants to reverse the image—to effeminate the male and make the female masculine. Such a transposition is contrary to God's plan. It is unnatural and, therefore, dissatisfying. Society strives to corrupt the male image and reduce him to a unisex creature. But in doing so, society tampers with social balance.

Within the animal kingdom, the male of the species differs from the female in his role. Always the aggressor, he is often the one with the beautiful feathers, the longer mane, and the more-colorful markings. God is not a male chauvinist, but these designs of the Creator have reason and purpose.

The male is designed with that godlike poise— that special appeal necessary to the law of attraction between the sexes. *Appeal* is not the created product of the entertainment world, the fashion industry, or the cosmetic companies. It is integral to creation. Why is this sense of majesty incorporated in the male? Because the *seed is in the male.*

All man-made or demon-designed religion seeks to elevate the female as deity. This Babylonian cult of "goddess" wars against God's revelation and mirrors the undertow of Satan's effort to substitute Eve for Adam.

"For Adam was first formed, then Eve. And Adam was not deceived, but the woman being deceived was in the transgression" (1 Timothy 2:13-14). When we meddle with the male image, we play into Satan's hands.

There is no question that our Savior was *male*— the Son of God. And He remains so. This does not make female the second-class gender. Woman is never to be considered lesser in value. Man is the reflection of God; woman is the reflection of man. The question is not one of equality but of *imagery.*

When we try to eliminate the distinction between male and female, we go against God's design. God wants us to maintain this distinction, especially within the marriage relationship.

This doesn't mean that only the wife washes the dishes and only the husband takes out the garbage. Sexual distinction has little to do with the assignment of tasks or the kind of job a person does. Jesus washed the feet of His disciples and cooked breakfast for them on the beach. Did that make Him any less a man?

Husbands must stand firm, however, against the trends of society to mold them into sexless jellyfish. At the same time, working wives must guard against becoming tough, aggressive go-getters whose jobs force their families into second place. God's original plan for marriage is a relationship in which the wife respects her husband as head of the family and the husband tenderly loves and provides for his wife.

When a husband fulfills his God-given male image in the home, and his wife supports that image, the proper balance is maintained. The result is marital and sexual bliss that comes close to paradise.

3. The Pharisees also came unto him, tempting him, and saying unto him, Is it lawful for a man to put away his wife for every cause?

4. And he answered and said unto them, Have ye not read, that he which made them at the beginning made them male and female,

5. And said, For this cause shall a man leave father and mother, and shall cleave to his wife: and they twain shall be one flesh?

6. Wherefore they are no more twain, but one flesh. What therefore God hath joined together, let not man put asunder.

7. They say unto him, Why did Moses then command to give a writing of divorcement, and to put her away?

8. He saith unto them, Moses because of the hardness of your hearts suffered you to put away your wives: but from the beginning it was not so.

7

CONSIDERING THE CONSEQUENCES

Ann Landers once asked her readers to answer this question: If you had it to do all over again, would you marry the same person? It was close. Of 50,000 persons who responded, 48 percent said yes, while 52 percent said no.

One husband wrote: "Marriage is the only war where you sleep with the enemy." Adam might have said that in the Garden of Eden. He did say, "The woman thou gavest to be with me, she . . ." (Genesis 3:12). Placing the blame on his wife was hardly cavalier, let alone spiritual.

Marriage has more built-in hazzards than the game of golf—a snoring partner, a live-in parent, financial difficulties, discipline problems with the kids, ad infinitum. Is marriage meant to be a tussle? Is it an obstacle course where survivors are decorated with Golden Wedding Anniversary honors?

In the United States today, approximately half of all marriages end in divorce. Our judicial system, in response to public sentiment, makes it easy. Look back through history. During Roman times, all a man had to do to divorce his wife was send her a note requesting that she remove her things from his house. In Chaldea, in Abram's time, a man could divorce his spouse by proclaiming, "Thou art not my wife."

Marriage is God's idea, but man devised the concept of divorce. "What therefore God hath joined together, let not man put asunder" (Matthew 19:6).

God built harmony and balance into His universe, and some things in the world belong together. They complement and strengthen each other—like stars in the sky, water in the ocean, and husbands with their wives. Confusion and chaos result when certain things are separated. Any division between couples and every cancellation of the marriage contract disturbs and damages God's order for His world.

Marriage sets boundaries for society. Without it there would be no basis for the home, the family, the community, or the nation. The alternative is an animal existence.

If the concept of marriage were eliminated, we would have the same conditions that existed in

Israel before they had a king: "Every man did that which was right in his own eyes" (Judges 17:6).

Our nation is on the verge of the same chaotic conditions. A rebellious cry is heard in the land today: "Let us break their bands asunder, and cast away their cords from us" (Psalm 2:3). No one wants to be bound by rules or have limitations placed on their "personal freedom."

Many people blame the church for setting up restrictions that interfere with an individual's quest for true happiness. That's like saying the coach of the football team hates the game because he demands that his players go by the rulebook. The coach loves playing the game—particularly when his team is winning.

God has put together a winning combination in marriage. And what God has joined together, man is foolish to separate.

Broken Promises

How long am I bound when I place my signature on the marriage license? Maybe it should come with a guarantee stating that my investment will be gladly refunded if, after thirty days, I am not completely satisfied. The apostle Paul says, "Art thou bound unto a wife? Seek not to be loosed" (1 Corinthians 7:27).

Paul admits, "He that is married careth for the

things that are of the world, how he may please his wife" (1 Corinthians 7:33). *Pleasing one another*—all authorities on marriage agree that this is the trigger. Can the contract continue—should it continue—if one contracting party ceases to make it his or her duty to "please" the other?

The marriage relationship must be for mutual advantage, or it is fantasy. Pressures are experienced in marriage, and adjustments must be made. Keeping such a delicate contract in force requires constant vigilance and effort on the part of both husband and wife. If the concept of marriage is worthy, then it is worth fighting for.

Society does not need more divorce settlements—it needs more superior living. It takes considerable courage to walk out, but it takes even greater courage to stay. "And having done all . . . stand!" (Ephesians 6:13). When I exchange vows and a kiss at the altar, I commit myself to prove something. I cannot run out on it without repudiation of that commitment.

The marriage vow is sacred and binding because I give my word to someone. "Thou shalt not bear false witness" (Exodus 20:16). Another person makes an investment on my word. This is my responsibility before God. I have promised. A promise is more than a piece of paper. It requires redemption.

How does God feel about broken covenants and unkept promises? "The Lord hath been witness between thee ... and the wife of thy covenant. ... For the Lord ... saith that he hateth putting away" (Malachi 2:14,16).

No one can doubt, in reading the Word, the preference of God in spite of what His mercy may allow. "Moses ... suffered you to put away your wives: but from the beginning it was not so" (Matthew 19:8). Divorce was never part of God's original design.

The Tragic Option

Maybe you have considered divorce as a possible option to a difficult marital situation. But to foster a casual attitude toward divorce is a biblical and spiritual mistake. Divorce is always a devastating, eroding experience with tragic consequences.

One man said the hardest thing for him after his divorce was to stop saying "we." He felt as though a deep unity had been split. The unity between husband and wife is meant to be a miracle, a splendor, a way of life. "For this cause shall a man leave father and mother, and shall cleave to his wife: and they twain shall be one flesh" (Matthew 19:5-6).

In most homes, there is a front door and a back door. Flowers are delivered to the front, and garbage leaves by the rear. In my profession, I have seen a lot of garbage. When dreams that were carried over the threshold with the bride crumble into ashes of disillusionment, they are tossed out like a wilted bouquet.

The smell of garbage reveals its contents. Moral, spiritual, and emotional disease breeds in the bitterness, the unfaithfulness, the cruelty—the wasted leftovers of a once-happy marriage.

Divorce is the result of something having turned sour. "Now the works of the flesh are manifest . . . adultery, forniction, uncleanness . . . hatred, variance, emulations, wrath, strife" (Galatians 5:19-20). Let's look into the ash heap of divorce and see what consequences smolder beneath the surface.

Divorce severes many long-established relationships—not only between the husband and wife but between in-laws, friends, social contacts, and children. The divorced become segregated from family members, and married friends look at them with suspicion. This severing leads to unbearable loneliness and isolation that can be the worst form of punishment for anyone. Only cheap comedy suggests divorce to be anything less than a deep wound. Often divorced men and women hide in tranquilizers and cry themselves to sleep at night.

Divorced people often feel angry or abandoned—sometimes for years. They can't resolve these feelings because they are cut off from the person who inflicted them. I've seen divorced men and women get so emotionally wretched they don't want to go on living.

Sin in spirit is as deadly as sin in the flesh; both can erode your health. High blood pressure and other physical problems are often caused by seething resentment and unforgiveness. Healing does not come by talking it out with the psychiatrist or marriage counselor. Healing takes place when the disagreeing parties put James 5:16 into practice: "Confess your faults one to another, and pray for one another, that ye may be healed."

Many divorced people suffer from *guilt.* What does God say about what I've done? Can I ever really justify my action? The pastor said it was all right. The court said it was legal. The relatives said I did the best thing. But you are not going to answer to the pastor, the court, or your relatives. You are going to stand before God, and you know it.

The very nature of divorce is meant to be final. It is not a pleasant "au revoir" or an "auf Wiedersehen."

Divorce is a tragedy, and the shock waves go in all directions.

Suffering The Consequences

Are there serious consequences to what may seem like a reasonable solution to your marital problems? Who suffers the most from divorce—mom, dad, or the kids?

Children experience enough stress outside the home without the added burden of a shattered family life that leaves them feeling defenseless. They may suffer in silence but not without devastating consequences. Divorce can never substitute for the balance (mom and dad) needed to raise children in a healthy environment.

The children of a divorce are thrust into their own maze of problems. They may feel like dad has deserted them, so they do not want to see him—but he has visiting privileges. This kind of situation creates unimagined tension and turmoil in a child.

Sometimes children are used as pawns in their parents' arguments. A conflict of loyalties results, and children have to deal with feelings of guilt and confusion.

Some parents abandon children simply because they consider their own needs more important than their children's welfare. "And whosoever shall offend one of these little ones . . . it is better for him [or her] that a millstone were hanged about his [or her] neck, and he [or she] were cast into the sea" (Mark 9:42). That's a serious consequence to a selfish solution.

Is divorce the example you want to set for your marriageable son or daughter? You pray that your children will inherit your strengths not your weaknesses, but some problems are hereditary. "Visiting the iniquity of the fathers upon the children unto the third and fourth generation" (Exodus 20:5). Do you want your children to inherit a legacy of divorce?

Long after the divorce is final, children still suffer the consequences. The child of the dissolved marriage, now a bride, announces she will have a church wedding. Mother will sit on the left front pew, of course. If dad comes, where should he sit—next or behind? Should father or step-father be in the receiving line? The repercussions affect the children of divorce for the remainder of their lives.

What about divorced fathers? Do they experience heartache? Involuntary absence is forced upon many husbands whose wives are bent on doing "their own thing." Being wrenched from children is excruciating anguish. While these dads yearn to see their children, they are held in legal custody by their former marital partner.

The divorced dad reacts like a person who has been robbed, and the emotional loss surfaces in unusual ways. He often suffers the terror of impending loss and fears a diminishing relationship with his own offspring. "Soon my child won't recognize me—won't even remember me." Who can calculate the effect losing a child has on a father's heart? His pent-up longings, in many cases, become unbearable, and child-napping can be the result.

The divorced woman faces a different problem. Divorce destroys the innocence and thrill of unsullied romance, leaving her craving for affection. At the same time, the divorced wife determines never again to expose herself to hurt. This makes her hard and insensitive in all her relationships with other people—both male and female, friends and family, children and adult.

Jesus knew the pressures faced by divorced women. He said whoever divorces his wife "causes her to commit adultery" (Matthew 5:32). A moral vulnerability develops in a woman whose ego and self-esteem are destroyed by rejection. She wants to know she is desirable, and her flesh cries out for proof.

To the woman at the well, Jesus said, "Go, call thy husband. . . . The woman answered and said, I have no husband. Jesus said . . . Thou hast had five husbands; and he whom thou now hast is not thy husband" (John 4:16-18). Our Lord knew and cited the trend that affects many divorced women.

Whatever the circumstances, and many are compelling, divorce involves damage. The consequences can be devastating to all concerned.

Paying The Price

Are you grieving, heartbroken, and torn by the problems in your marriage? I point you to Jesus. "He is . . . acquainted with grief" (Isaiah 53:3). He understands the vacant chair and sympathizes with the child's question that defies any professional answer. Jesus is there in the lonely hour.

Is there an option other than divorce?

One pastor, dealing with the problem of divorce, wrote:

> I received a letter from a couple who had the most hopeless marriage I've ever seen. But they wouldn't give up. They kept asking for help and wouldn't stop trying to make their marriage work.

129

when things began to mend, it wasn't easy. They experienced slips and restarts.

But this couple acknowledged their own weaknesses (without losing sight of their strengths). Finally, they have reached the point where they are looking for and admiring the good things in each other—things they had blacked out before they learned to pray together. They are growing spiritually, and their love is increasing. They have paid a price, but, taking everything into account, it hasn't cost them as much as a divorce.

This pastor put his finger on the *option*. I believe it is the business of the church to offer and stress the option of sticking it out and making the marriage work. The consequences will be far less damaging than those brought on by divorce.

A healthy marriage cannot grow in an environment of competition, hatred, boasting, jealousy, low self-esteem, or verbal abuse. These weeds are inherent in the Adamic soil and can stifle love and communication. But pulling out the weeds won't do any good unless the soil is different. The solution is to work at changing the climate.

Maybe your marriage is more like two becoming two instead of two becoming one. Divorce may seem to be the only answer at this point. But I urge you to consider the option of working to hold your marriage together. Although you alone may have to put forth most of the effort for a while, don't give up. With God's help and your persistence, the two of you can become one again.

1. And the third day there was a marriage in Cana of Galilee; and the mother of Jesus was there:

2. And both Jesus was called, and his disciples, to the marriage.

3. And when they wanted wine, the mother of Jesus saith unto him, They have no wine. . . .

7. Jesus saith unto them, Fill the waterpots with water. And they filled them up to the brim.

8. And he saith unto them, Draw out now, and bear unto the governor of the feast. And they bare it.

9. When the ruler of the feast had tasted the water that was made wine, and knew not whence it was: (but the servants which drew the water knew;) the governor of the feast called the bridegroom,

10. And saith unto him, Every man at the beginning doth set forth good wine; and when men have well drunk, then that which is worse: but thou hast kept the good wine until now.

8
MAKING MARRIAGE LAST

Marriage is like a championship golf course—obstacles appear at every turn. Although you know they are out there when you tee off, you still hope to avoid the sand traps and the duck ponds. But when they trap you, don't quit. Instead call upon God and use every skill you have to escape. If you get a "bogey" on one hole, you don't give up. You expect a "birdie" on the next!

The apostle Paul has this advice: "Not as though I had already attained, either were already perfect ... but this one thing I do ... reaching forth unto those things which are before, I press toward the mark" (Philippians 3:12-14).

Building a permanent partnership takes daily effort. Marriage is like a garden. If left unattended and uncultured, it will quickly return to weeds. Couples must constantly set goals for themselves and their relationship.

The vows you repeated on your wedding day included the words "to have and to hold from this day forward." Once you have your mate, the responsibility for holding him or her belongs to you.

My wife Dorothy and I have been married nearly sixty years. We have survived the stresses of daily life and the strains of building a meaningful relationship. From the start of our marriage, Dorothy and I determined to make the best of every situation.

Our marriage has been like baseball. We have always kept in mind that there are nine innings to a ballgame—and sometimes more. When things got tough, we believed that victory could come in any inning. "For we are saved by hope" (Romans 8:24). Hope is the necessary ingredient in any marriage to keep it from unraveling and to make it last.

Lasting Secrets

What happens long after passion and romance have cooled—when dishwashing and toting the garbage have become major issues? How do couples stay together?

You *work* at marriage! This does not imply stress and strain but putting forth an *effort*. It means effort in dress, management, entertainment, and adjustment of your rights as an individual. These investments bring rich dividends later. Let's examine a few practical ways you can give your marriage that enduring quality.

1. *Enjoy being together.*

Spending time with one another gives your relationship that special quality of durability. The jewel of *presence*—just knowing your mate is around—brings precious comfort.

Working on special projects together creates unity of purpose and oneness in goals. Determine to discover every possible area of common interest. As the years go by, simple pleasures like gardening and walking, shopping and travel, reading and conversation take on new meaning—especially if you enjoy them together.

Dorothy and I relax together by attending well-performed musicals or concerts. Over the years our preferences in music have merged. We can enjoy quietly listening to a renowned philharmonic playing "Evening Star" from Tannenhauser or get excited when the Marine Band strikes out a lively march.

Eating out is another one of our favorite activities. Dorothy and I both love excellent cuisine. Going to a fancy restaurant where we have to dress for the occasion brings us great pleasure.

Where you go and what you do matters little. Being together is what counts. Any marriage that is going to last has to be one in which a husband and wife make an effort to do things as a couple.

Finding mutual interests, however, may take some bending on both sides. A wife whose husband likes to play golf may have to take lessons so she can join him on Saturday mornings. Browsing through antique shops may not be a husband's idea of a good time, but any man can learn to appreciate the quality of older furniture.

⌐Neglect can destroy a relationship.⌐ The Bible asks a very thought-provoking question, "How shall we escape, if we neglect. . . ?" (Hebrews 2:3). Don't allow neglect to eat away at the fiber of your marriage. Instead, escape the divorce court by tightening the cords of your relationship with togetherness.

2. *Share responsibilities.*

In any successful marriage, responsibilities and duties must be shared by both partners. Winners work together. A husband wins by making the bed while his wife prepares breakfast. A wife who is a good cook and a smart housekeeper will always be a winner in her husband's eyes. Offering to take out the garbage or balance the checkbook—

without being asked—eliminates nagging and harrassment.

Sharing responsibility for your children adds permanence to the husband/wife relationship. Children and grandchildren contribute to the joy of married life and cement a couple together in a way nothing else can. In addition to your own little unit, the extended family of grandparents and relatives is also important. *Roots* make strong trees, and families need to be interlocked like the root system holding up a giant oak.

To fully interpret the word "helpmeet" takes time. In the first years of marriage, each partner is inclined to help himself or herself foremost. Later the ideal is realized—the helping of each other. Selfishness yields to selflessness.

At a gala banquet given in my honor after twenty-five years of ministry on the American Broadcasting Network, Dorothy said these immortal words, "For me these twenty-five years have meant a tired preacher and a suitcase full of dirty clothes!" My career had brought little glamor to Dorothy's life, but she was always there for me, behind the scenes, meeting my needs in simple and practical ways.

A seasoned marriage is no longer a physical contest involving the survival of the fittest. As boundaries are erased, she may become his eyes;

he may become her legs. Helping each other is beauty in full bloom. Nothing in the tawdry rough-and-tumble world compares to a marriage in which the partners are dependent on one another.

3. *Establish common values.*

Without common values it is difficult to hold any relationship together. Personal convictions, if not shared, should at least be respected by the other partner. Attending church as a family, reading God's Word together, and praying for each other are absolutely necessary practices if common values are to be established in your marriage.

My wife and I can trust each other's judgment because we hold common values in the areas of finance and spiritual beliefs. Every couple needs to determine certain boundaries for their life together. Dorothy and I have kept our "rules of marriage" to a few:

a. Never go to sleep without settling a disagreement.

b. Dorothy manages the money.

c. When led by the Spirit to contribute to some agency of the Church, neither partner needs to consult the other.

In our marriage, we have established God's *priority:* "But seek ye first the kingdom of God, and his righteousness; and all these things shall be added unto you" (Matthew 6:33). The adhesive that keeps a husband and wife together is *putting God first.*

Fellowship with other Christian couples helps cement common values and keeps the pressures of the world in perspective. Like the wedding at Cana, a good marriage must include "both Jesus . . . and his disciples" (John 2:1-2). Marriage should start in the Lord's presence and be nurtured among the disciples—fellow-believers.

As you move closer to the final horizon, you reach out for more meaning to life. The bravado of "I haven't time for church" or "praying is for cowards" fades. Common spiritual values provide the strength and endurance needed as the finish line approaches.

4. *Don't take one another for granted.*

Slovenly habits and sloppy appearance can produce a tedious and tasteless relationship. A wife who neglects her figure, hair, and dress is asking for loneliness and divorce. A husband who ceases to be attentive and who becomes careless in personal hygiene is asking for grief and desertion.

Even with Bible in hand, a woman can't expect to hold onto her man if she allows herself to become dowdy. A wife's prayers will bounce off the ceiling if she foolishly lets her once beautiful body slink into obesity.

Some women use becoming pregnant and giving birth to children as their excuse for gaining weight. You may be the mother of his children, but you are his wife as well. Don't trade one role for another and end up taking your husband for granted.

Keep your body in good shape. It's never too late for a makeover. Like vintage cars or antique furniture, your physical condition can be improved with work and determination. Many helps are available today to enhance the outward appearance. With a little extra effort, you can achieve the same attraction for one another that you had during courtship.

"Godliness with contentment is great gain" (1 Timothy 6:6), but a laizze-faire attitude that succumbs to the status quo is neither godly nor contented. *Complacency* is your deadly enemy. Don't let the razor become dull or the lipstick dry up. Learn how to please one another in your physical appearance.

The law of attraction depends upon adherence. To *have* you must *hold*. Every day you must hold your mate's attention. The competition is tough, and it never ceases. You can't put a padlock on your marriage to keep your spouse from escaping.

But you can make him or her a "prisoner of love." That may sound ruthless, but a husband and wife have to use every means available to ward off the enemies of their marriage.

In any attack, Satan enlists two allies: the *world* and the *flesh*. The world system, appealing to the flesh, is the enemy of every marriage. "For all that is in the world, the lust of the flesh, and the lust of the eyes, and the pride of life, is not of the Father, but is of the world" (1 John 2:16). Lust, ambition, and pride are the weapons Satan uses to destroy the special unity between a husband and wife.

You can protect your marriage by keeping your guard up. Marriage is not an isolated union surrounded by walls like a monastery. Marriage is a contest, and the losers are the ones who take their spouses for granted.

Be a fighter. Get in the ring and win. Wives, don't sit back and let your husband slip through your fingers while you lounge around watching soap operas and eating potato chips. Husbands, pay attention to your wife before she finds someone who *will* send her flowers and take her out to dinner.

Making marriage last is a full-time job. But the pay is good, and the benefits are great. What have you got to lose?

5. *Keep the excitement in your marriage.*

Like new wine, one of the most difficult achievements in marriage is keeping the intoxication in it. Over the years, the excitement disappears. Preventing this from happening is probably the greatest of all miracles and requires divine intervention.

Jesus turned the water into wine, and He can turn a tasteless, colorless marriage into a vibrant, exciting, and fulfilling experience. The miracle of a happy marriage *can* and *does* happen.

When you see your spouse, do your eyes light up? Does the color flow to your cheeks? Are you excited to be with him or her?

When the thrilling mystery in marriage is gone, you end up just going through the motions. Sexual intimacy with your mate need not decay to a drab, repulsive, or escape experience. Like currency, the possibilities are unlimited—but it's up to you and your spouse to discover new ways to entice one another. Preserving the excitement in marriage is the secret to making "the wedding night" last and last.

Keep your relationship as exciting as it was during the honeymoon. Maintain the flutter and the tingle; keep the adrenalin flowing. The feelings may be lying dormant, but it's up to you to wake them up and keep them activated.

Sweeter As The Years Go By

"Thou hast kept the good wine until now" (John 2:10). Wine is not the only property whose value increases with age. Some people think the early years of marriage are the best, but God intends the "good wine" for later.

Like a pair of shoes you have worn for years or a chair you have molded to your body, marriage becomes more comfortable as the years go by. In a time-worn marriage, there is more humor and more understanding between husband and wife.

"Sweeter as the years go by" is not a myth. As time passes, the inclusion of children, grandchildren, and great-grandchildren escalates the excitement of marriage. Investments begin to pay, and economic pressures lessen. Couples have more time for leisure and can enjoy travel, hobbies, reading, and entertainment.

Back in the days of network radio, one of the most popular programs was Major Bowes' *Original Amateur Hour*. Many of the amateurs featured on his show later became famous stars in the entertainment industry. Major Bowes' greatest achievement, however, was not his discovery of talented entertainers—it was his marriage. He said of his wife:

"I hope she may live a thousand years,
And I, a thousand less one day:
So that I may never know she has
passed away."

Marriage is like an unfolding rose. The bud is desirable, but the full glory and scent come later. I have found this to be true in my relationship with Dorothy.

In a marriage, the sunset years are the best. Any artist will tell you that *sunsets* are preferable to sunrises. Both are glorious miracles. But nothing photographed or placed on canvas can equal the color, dazzle, variety, and sense of peace created by a sunset. It is truly a tragedy that so few marriages reach this golden time of life.

May you and your mate learn the secrets of making your marriage last, so you can walk into the sunset together—not as two, but as one.